The Cottage at Cardiff
QUILTS

You can almost see the California sunshine in Kathy Cardiff's quilts! Plenty of fun piecing and a bit of artful appliqué make these heirloom-quality bed covers, wall hangings, and lap quilts a joy to sew. The ten designs include sweet features like scalloped edges, pieced and appliquéd flowers, easy Nine-Patch blocks, or a whirl of pinwheels. Refresh your creative spirit by making these fresh quilts from Cardiff Farms. You'll love having their natural beauty in your home!

LEISURE ARTS, INC.
Little Rock, Arkansas

The designer of these breathtaking quilts is the talented Kathy Cardiff, who lives on the family-operated Cardiff Farms in California. Her husband tends the three-acre farm and its promising young orchard while Kathy develops new quilts for her pattern business. Sewing is a longtime passion for Kathy.

"I learned to sew from my mother at a very young age, as she was an accomplished seamstress," Kathy says. "I always loved the way quilts make a home feel warm and inviting but didn't really have the opportunity to make my own until my two children were out of school. In 2001, I retired from our family business and took a few quilting classes. I fell in love with quilting and consider it the perfect outlet for my creativity. In 2006, I decided to get more serious and turn it into a business.

"My quilting studio is on our property, and it's filled with antiques and fabric that I use for inspiration. "I do receive some help with the business. My good friend Peggy Egger beautifully machine-quilts all of my samples. And in recent years as the business has grown, my daughter Taylor has taken over the financial and technical side of things.

"Besides quilting, one of my favorite things to do is preserve the foods we grow and use them in our everyday recipes. To really relax, I love taking a day just for gardening! I maintain all of the flower and organic vegetable gardens at Cardiff Farms, which are mostly for family use. I feel completely refreshed after spending an entire day outside getting my hands dirty. After that, I'm ready to start quilting again the next day."

See more of Kathy's lovely quilt patterns at TheCottageAtCardiffFarms.com. Kathy also teaches quilt and sewing classes several times a month at The Country Loft in La Mesa, California.

Table of contents

Boston Tea Party
quilt

This quilt was inspired by one of my traditional favorites called "Boston Commons." This version is made from larger squares than the original and goes together very quickly. It can be made from only two colors for a vintage look or many lights and colors for a scrappy look. The quilt shown is made from several contrasting colors and one fabric for all the light sections.

Finished Quilt Size:
77³/₈" x 83³/₄" (197 cm x 213 cm)
Finished Block Size:
4¹/₂" x 4¹/₂" (11 cm x 11 cm)

YARDAGE REQUIREMENTS

Yardage is based on 43"/44" (109 cm/112 cm) wide fabric with a usable width of 40" (102 cm). A fat quarter measures approximately 18" x 22" (46 cm x 56 cm) and yields twelve 5" x 5" (13 cm x 13 cm) squares.

> 154 assorted light-colored squares 5" x 5" (13 cm x 13 cm) from charm packs. Squares can also be cut from 14 assorted fat quarters **or** 3¹/₈ yds (2.9 m) *total* of assorted print fabrics.
> 134 assorted medium- to dark-colored squares 5" x 5" (13 cm x 13 cm) from charm packs. Squares can also be cut from 12 assorted fat quarters **or** 2⁵/₈ yds (2.4 m) *total* of assorted print fabrics.
> 7¹/₈ yds (6.5 m) of fabric for backing
> ⁷/₈ yd (80 cm) of fabric for binding

You will also need:

> 85³/₈" x 91³/₄" (217 cm x 233 cm) piece of batting

ASSEMBLING THE QUILT TOP

*Follow **Machine Piecing**, page 84, and **Pressing**, page 85. Use a scant ¹/₄" seam allowance.*

*The arrows under each Row of the **Quarter Section Diagram**, page 8, indicate which direction to press the seam allowances for each seam. The arrows between the Rows indicate which way to press the seam allowances once those two rows have been joined.*

1. This quilt is assembled in four sections. Refer to **Quarter Section Diagram** to assemble a Quarter Section. Begin by sewing the squares in the longest row together first. That will be **Row L**.
2. Sew the squares together to make **Row K**. If you lay Row L near your sewing machine you will be able to check your placement of color so you don't put the same colors together.

Continued on page 8.

Boston Tea Party continued.

3. Sew Row K to Row L, keeping the left edge even. You will notice that each row gets one block shorter until you reach **Row A**, which is one single square.

4. Continue assembling Rows and sewing Rows together until you have joined all 12 Rows to make Section 1. Congratulations! One section is complete.

5. To make Section 2, omit Row L and begin with Row K. To make it a little easier, cover the bottom Row on the diagram with a sheet of paper until a few Rows have been sewn.

6. Continue assembling Rows and sewing Rows together to complete Section 2. Refer to **Quilt Top Assembly Diagram** to align left edges and sew Sections 1 and 2 together. Press the seam allowance toward Section 2. Yeah! Half of your quilt is complete!

7. Repeat Steps 1-6 to make remaining Sections 1 and 2. Sew these 2 sections together.

8. Refer to **Quilt Top Assembly Diagram** to sew halves together.

Quarter Section Diagram

Quilt Top Assembly Diagram

QUILTING AND BINDING

*To make binding this quilt a little simpler, you might choose to cut off the zigzag edge and just have a quilt with straight sides. If so, quilt first and then trim off the points. If you cut it before you quilt you will be exposing a bias edge which will stretch easily and distort your quilt. If you choose to make a quilt with straight sides, you can use **Continuous Bias Strip Binding**, page 90, or **Straight-Grain Binding**, page 91.*

1. Follow **Quilting**, page 86, to mark, layer, and quilt. My quilt is machine quilted with an all-over meandering flower pattern.

2. Cut a 27" x 27" square from fabric for binding. Follow **Making Continuous Bias Strip Binding**, page 90, Steps 1-7, to make 480" of 1$^1/_4$"w bias binding. Press 1 long dge of binding $^1/_4$" to wrong side. Follow **Attaching Binding with Mitered Corners**, page 92, to attach binding to quilt, pivoting at inner corners.

Sunshine and Blue
wall hanging

This project was made from two different types of fabric. I used cotton fabric for the pieced front and the backing and wonderful wool for the appliqués. Wool comes in so many beautiful colors and is perfect for appliqué. I added the borders to the background and then layered and quilted the quilt. I then stitched on my wool pieces with a primitive whipstitch to create my picture.

You have so many options when it comes to threads and stitches that you can get creative and make a one-of-a-kind treasure for your home or a gift for a very good friend.

Finished Quilt Size:
29" x 41" (74 cm x 104 cm)

YARDAGE REQUIREMENTS

Yardage is based on 43"/44" (109 cm/112 cm) wide fabric with a usable width of 40" (102 cm) for cotton fabrics. A fat quarter measures approximately 18" x 22" (46 cm x 56 cm).

Cotton Fabrics

$15^1/_2$" x $27^1/_2$" (39 cm x 70 cm) piece of black/tan stripe fabric for background

10 assorted black/tan print fat quarters for inner border and middle pieced border *(**Note:** There will be enough left over to use for scrappy binding and a pieced backing, if desired.)*

$^1/_2$ yd (46 cm) of black/tan print fabric for outer border

$1^1/_2$ yds (1.4 m) of fabric for backing unless piecing from remainder of fat quarters

Wool Fabrics

10" x 16" (25 cm x 41 cm) piece of grey #1 for can

3" x 7" (8 cm x 18 cm) piece of grey #2 for can accents

6" x 7" (15 cm x 18 cm) piece **each** of 2 yellows for flowers

3" x 3" (8 cm x 8 cm) piece of black for flower centers

1" x 12" (3 cm x 30 cm) piece of dark olive for stems

4" x 7" (10 cm x 18 cm) piece **each** of 2 dark olives for leaves

7" x 7" (18 cm x 18 cm) piece **each** of 3 greens for leaves

2" x 12" (5 cm x 30 cm) piece of brown for berry branches

4" x 6" (10 cm x 15 cm) piece of lime green for berries

6" x 7" (15 cm x 18 cm) piece of blue for berries

Continued on page 14.

Sunshine and Blue continued.

You will also need:

37" x 49" (94 cm x 124 cm) piece of batting

Freezer paper **or** Steam-a-Seam 2® fusible web, depending on desired appliqué technique (See page 15.)

Embroidery floss and/or pearl cotton*

*Designer used Valdani 100% colorfast hand-dyed pearl cotton in sizes 8 and 12

CUTTING THE PIECES

*Follow **Rotary Cutting**, page 82, to cut fabric. Borders include extra length for "insurance" and will be trimmed after assembling quilt top center. All measurements include ¼" seam allowances.*

From black/tan print fat quarters:

- Choose 1 fat quarter for inner border. From this fat quarter:
  - Cut 5 **inner border strips** 1" x 22".
  - Cut 3 **strips** 1½" x 22" for middle border.
  - Cut 1 **binding strip** 2½" x 22" for scrappy binding.
- From *each* of the remaining fat quarters:
  - Cut 3 **strips** 1½" x 22" for middle border.
  - Cut 1 **binding strip** 2½" x 22" for scrappy binding

From black/tan print fabric for outer border:

- Cut 2 **side outer borders** 3½" x 38½".
- Cut 2 **top/bottom outer borders** 3½" x 32½".

ASSEMBLING THE QUILT TOP

*Follow **Machine Piecing**, page 84, and **Pressing**, page 85. Use a scant ¼" seam allowance.*

1. Sew **inner border strips** together end to end. Cut 2 side inner borders 1" x 31½". Cut 2 top/bottom inner borders 1" x 20½". Follow **Adding Squared Borders**, page 86, to add **inner borders** to **background**.

2. For middle border, sew 3 different black/tan print **strips** together to make **Strip Set**. Press all seam allowances in the same direction. Make 10 Strip Sets. Cut across Strip Sets at 1½" intervals to make a total of 100 **Unit 1's**.

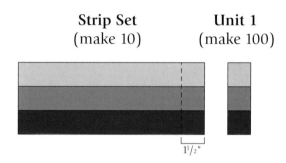

Strip Set (make 10)   **Unit 1** (make 100)

1½"

3. Matching long edges and alternating the direction of the seam allowance, sew 28 **Unit 1's** together to make **Side Middle Border**. Really mix the Unit 1's for a very scrappy look. Make 2 Side Middle Borders.

4. In same manner, sew 22 **Unit 1's** together to make **Top Middle Border**. Repeat to make **Bottom Middle Border**.

5. Sew Side Middle Borders to quilt top center. Sew Top and Bottom Middle Borders to quilt top center.

6. Follow **Adding Squared Borders**, page 86, to add **side**, then **top** and **bottom outer borders** to quilt top.

QUILTING AND BINDING

1. Follow **Quilting**, page 86, to mark, layer, and quilt. My quilt is machine quilted with diagonal crosshatch quilting across the background, quilting in the ditch along each border, straight-line quilting through each row of squares in the middle border and in the outer border.
2. Follow **Making Straight-Grain Binding**, page 91, and use **binding strips** to make binding. Follow **Attaching Binding with Mitered Corners**, page 92, to attach binding to quilt.

ADDING THE APPLIQUÉS

Choose freezer paper technique or Steam-a-Seam 2 technique, right, and use patterns, pages 17-19, for appliqué. The patterns are printed in reverse.

From grey #1 wool fabric:
- Cut **pitcher**.
- Cut **handle** $1/2$" x 15"

From grey #2 wool fabric:
- Cut **top accent** $1/4$" x $2^3/4$".
- Cut **bottom accent**.

From yellow wool fabrics:
- Cut a *total* of 28 **flower petals** as desired.

From black wool fabric:
- Cut 3 **centers**.

From dark olive wool fabric:
- Cut 3 **stems** $1/4$" x 12".

From dark olive and green wool fabrics:
- Cut a *total* of 65 **small leaves**.
- Cut a *total* of 9 **large leaves**.

From brown wool fabric:
- Cut 4 **berry branches** $1/8$" x 12".

From lime green wool fabric:
- Cut 22 **berries**.

From blue wool fabric:
- Cut 42 **berries**.

Freezer Paper Technique

1. Trace all pattern pieces onto the dull side of the freezer paper. Roughly cut out the pattern pieces and press them, shiny side down, to the wrong side of the wools chosen for those pieces. Cut out pieces on drawn lines with sharp scissors. For narrow pieces, such as branches, vines, and stems, cut the freezer paper to the size of the wool piece. Iron freezer paper to wool and use rotary cutter and ruler to cut pieces according to measurements.
2. Remove the freezer paper from all pieces. Lay pieces on background in order from the background to the foreground. Trim the stems to the desired lengths. Secure the pieces on the background with appliqué pins.
3. Using your favorite embroidery floss and/or pearl cotton, stitch the pieces in place. I used a primitive Whipstitch. A Blanket Stitch also looks nice, but you can use any of your favorite stitches as long as all edges are secured in place.

Steam-a-Seam 2® Technique

1. Trace all pattern pieces onto the paper side of the fusible web that has the web stuck to it. Trace patterns to be cut from the same fabric as close together as possible and as many times as indicated in project instructions. This will save waste of the fusible and the fabric.
2. Roughly cut out the pattern pieces to be fused from like fabric and follow manufacturer's instructions to fuse web to the wrong side of the fabric chosen for those pieces. Do not remove paper backing. Repeat for all fabric pieces. Cut out pieces on drawn lines with sharp scissors.

3. For narrow pieces, such as branches, vines, and stems, cut the fusible web to the size of the wool piece. Iron fusible web to wool and use rotary cutter and ruler to cut pieces according to measurements.

4. Remove paper backing from all pieces. Lay pieces on background in order from the background to the foreground. Trim the stems to the desired lengths. Do not fuse any appliqués until you have completed the layout. When satisfied with placement, fuse appliqués in place.

5. Using your favorite embroidery floss and/or pearl cotton and being careful not to stitch through all layers, stitch the pieces in place. I used a primitive Whipstitch. A Blanket Stitch also looks nice, but you can use any of your favorite stitches as long as all edges are secured in place.

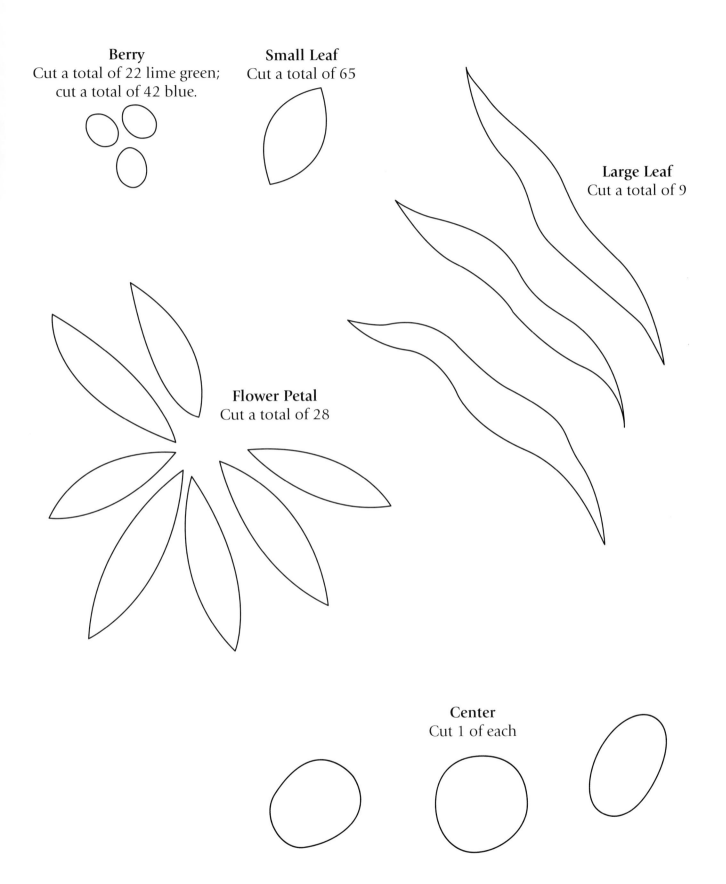

Berry
Cut a total of 22 lime green;
cut a total of 42 blue.

Small Leaf
Cut a total of 65

Large Leaf
Cut a total of 9

Flower Petal
Cut a total of 28

Center
Cut 1 of each

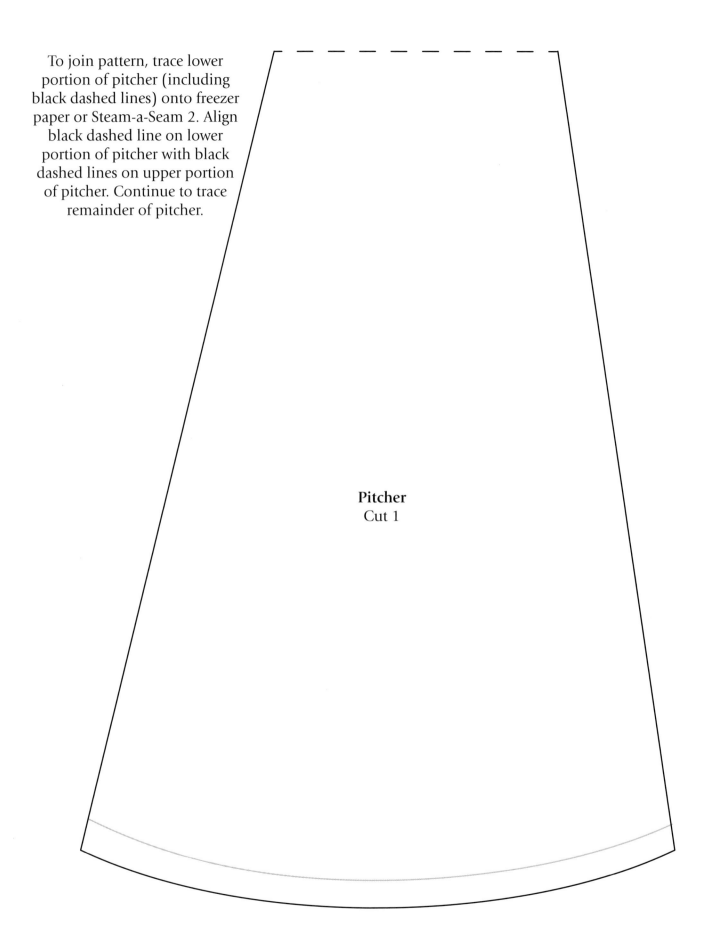

To join pattern, trace lower portion of pitcher (including black dashed lines) onto freezer paper or Steam-a-Seam 2. Align black dashed line on lower portion of pitcher with black dashed lines on upper portion of pitcher. Continue to trace remainder of pitcher.

Pitcher
Cut 1

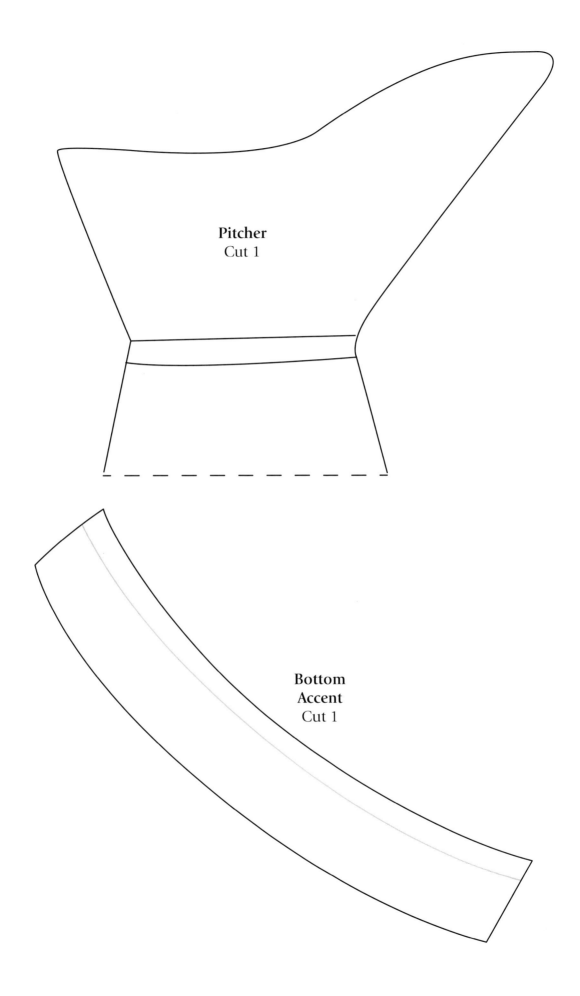

Pitcher
Cut 1

Bottom
Accent
Cut 1

Simply Charming
quilt

This quilt is made up of eighty-eight 5" Charm Squares. I used 3 large Charm Packs. I had some squares left over and used them for making some of the leaves and flowers. In addition, I added yardage for the borders, appliqué, back, and binding.

Finished Quilt Size:
 51" x 64¹/₂" (130 cm x 164 cm)
Finished Block Size:
 4¹/₂" x 4¹/₂" (11 cm x 11 cm)

Yardage Requirements, below, are given for fat quarters but 5" x 5" charm squares would make it go even faster.

YARDAGE REQUIREMENTS

Yardage is based on 43"/44" (109 cm/112 cm) wide fabric with a usable width of 40" (102 cm). A fat quarter measures approximately 18" x 22" (46 cm x 56 cm) and yields twelve 5" x 5" (13 cm x 13 cm) squares.

112 assorted print squares 5" x 5" (13 cm x 13 cm) from charm packs. Squares can also be cut from 5 light print fat quarters and 6 dark print fat quarters (1 brown, 2 greens, 1 purple, and 2 dark raspberry).
⁵/₈ yd (57 cm) of green print fabric for vines and leaves
¹/₄ yd (23 m) of dark print fabric for inner border
1¹/₄ yds (1.1 m) of light print fabric for outer border
4¹/₈ yds (3.8 m) of fabric for backing
⁵/₈ yd (57 cm) of fabric for binding
You will also need:
59" x 72¹/₂" (150 cm x 184 cm) piece of batting
Lightweight sew-in interfacing
¹/₄" (6 mm) bias tape maker

CUTTING THE PIECES

*Follow **Rotary Cutting**, page 82, to cut fabric. Cut all strips across the selvage-to-selvage width of the fabric unless otherwise indicated. Borders include extra length for "insurance" and will be trimmed after assembling quilt top center. All measurements include ¹/₄" seam allowances.*

If using fat quarters:
- From light print fat quarters, cut 44 assorted **squares** 5" x 5".
- From brown print fat quarter, cut 11 assorted **squares** 5" x 5".
- From green print fat quarters, cut 24 assorted **squares** 5" x 5". Set aside 13 squares for leaves.
- From purple print fat quarter, cut 12 assorted **squares** 5" x 5". Set aside 1 square for flower centers.
- From dark raspberry print fat quarters, cut 21 assorted **squares** 5" x 5". Set aside 10 squares for flowers.

From green print fabric for vines and leaves:
- Cut a 17" x 17" square. Follow **Making Continuous Bias Strip Binding**, page 90, to make 245" of 1"w continuous bias strip. Use bias tape maker to make ¹/₄"w vines.

From dark print fabric for inner borders:
- Cut 2 **side inner borders** 1¹/₂" x 53¹/₂", pieced as needed.
- Cut 2 **top/bottom inner borders** 1¹/₂" x 42¹/₂", pieced as needed.

From light print fabric for outer borders:
- Cut 2 **side outer borders** 6¹/₂" x 55¹/₂", pieced as needed.
- Cut 2 **top/bottom outer borders** 6¹/₂" x 54¹/₂", pieced as needed.

From fabric for binding:
- Cut 7 **binding strips** 2¹/₂"w.

Continued on page 24.

ASSEMBLING THE QUILT TOP

*Follow **Machine Piecing**, page 84, and **Pressing**, page 85. Use a scant ¹/₄" seam allowance.*

1. Refer to **Chain Piecing**, page 85, to sew 5" squares together in pairs - one light and one dark. Make 44 pairs. Press seam allowances toward the dark fabrics.
2. Now sew 4 pairs together to form a **Row** remembering to continue the light, dark, light, dark pattern. Make 11 Rows. Press seam allowances toward the dark fabrics.
3. Sew the Rows together to make quilt top center. Rotate Rows so that all odd numbered Rows begin with a dark print square and all even numbered Rows begin with a light print square. Press seam allowances toward the bottom of the quilt top center.
4. Follow **Adding Squared Borders**, page 86, to add **side**, then **top** and **bottom inner borders** to quilt top center.
5. In same manner, add **outer borders** to quilt top center.

PREPARING THE APPLIQUÉS

To prepare each appliqué, trace the desired pattern, page 25, onto interfacing with a permanent pen. Place on right side of fabric and sew on line with very, very small stitches (Twenty stitches to the inch or 1.8 on most machines works well.) Trim ¹/₈" outside stitching line and clip any curves. On the back of the shape, make a small slit in the interfacing and turn right side out; press carefully.

From remaining green print 5" x 5" squares and green print yardage:
- Cut 28 of *each* **leaf**.

From remaining purple print 5" x 5" squares:
- Cut 10 **flower centers**.

From remaining dark raspberry print 5" x 5" squares:
- Cut 10 **flowers**.

ADDING THE APPLIQUÉS

1. Arrange vine and appliqués on quilt top; pin in place.
2. Blindstitch vine and appliqués in place.

QUILTING AND BINDING

1. Follow **Quilting**, page 86, to mark, layer, and quilt. My quilt is machine quilted with a meandering flower pattern in the quilt top center and echo quilting around the vine and appliqués in the border.
2. Follow **Making Straight-Grain Binding**, page 91, and use **binding strips** to make binding. Follow **Attaching Binding with Mitered Corners**, page 92, to attach binding to quilt.

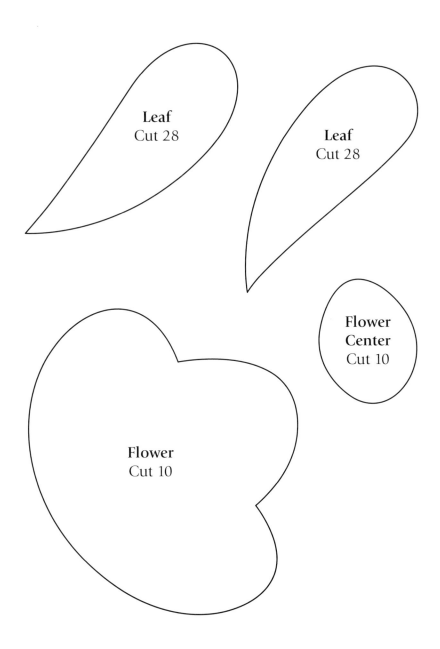

Leaf
Cut 28

Leaf
Cut 28

Flower Center
Cut 10

Flower
Cut 10

Buttercream & Sprinkles quilt

I think this is one of the fastest, easiest quilt tops I've ever put together. You can use as few as two or as many different colors as you desire. I used charm squares, but whether you are making it from charm packs or fat quarters, the cutting is minimal and the sewing is quite simple. Very few seams in this project have to match and that makes it go even quicker.

The color combination is entirely up to you. You can make all of your 9-Patch blocks the same or make every one a little bit different. How you place your darks and lights will change the entire look of the top. I have yet to see a color combo I didn't like. They all turn out beautifully!

Finished Quilt Size:
54" x 54" (137 cm x 137 cm)
Finished Block Size:
13" x 13" (33 cm x 33 cm)

YARDAGE REQUIREMENTS

*Yardage is based on 43"/44" (109 cm/112 cm)
wide fabric with a usable width of 40" (102 cm).
A fat quarter measures approximately 18" x 22"
(46 cm x 56 cm) and yields twelve 5" x 5"
(13 cm x 13 cm) squares.*

    81 assorted 5" x 5" (13 cm x 13 cm) squares
      from charm packs. Squares can also be cut
      from 7 or more assorted fat quarters.

    $1^5/_8$ yds (1.5 m) of light print fabric
      for border

    $3^1/_2$ yds (3.2 m) of fabric for backing

    $^5/_8$ yd (57 cm) of fabric for binding

You will also need:

    62" x 62" (157 cm x 157 cm) piece
      of batting

    Template plastic

    Water-soluble fabric marking pen

CUTTING THE PIECES

*Follow **Rotary Cutting**, page 82, to cut fabric. Cut all
strips across the selvage-to-selvage width of the fabric
unless otherwise indicated. Borders include extra length
for "insurance" and will be trimmed after assembling
quilt top center. All measurements include $^1/_4$" seam
allowances.*

From light print fabric for borders:

- Cut 2 *lengthwise* **side border strips**
  $7^1/_2$" x $43^1/_2$".
- Cut 2 *lengthwise* **top/bottom border
  strips** $7^1/_2$" x $57^1/_2$".

From fabric for binding:

- Cut a 20" x 20" square. Follow **Making
  Continuous Bias Strip Binding**, page 90,
  Steps 1-7, to make 240" of $1^1/_4$"w continuous
  bias strip.

Continued on page 30.

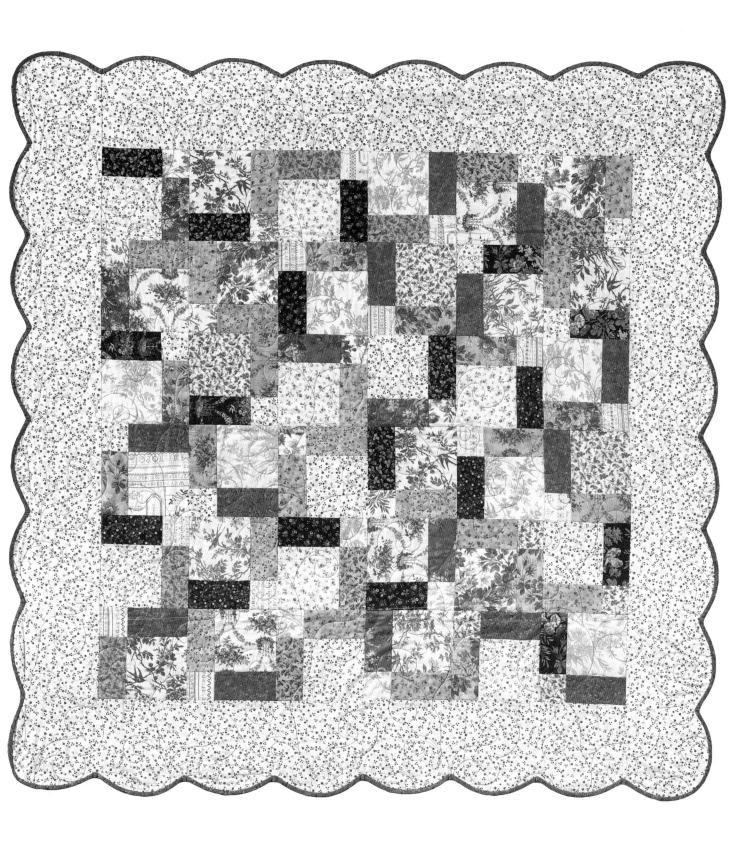

Buttercream and Sprinkles continued.

ASSEMBLING THE BLOCKS
*Follow **Machine Piecing**, page 84, and **Pressing**, page 85. Use a scant ¹/₄" seam allowance.*

1. Sew 3 squares together to make a Row. Make 3 Rows. Press seam allowances on 2 Rows toward the center square. Press seam allowances on remaining Row away from the center square. Alternating seam allowances, sew Rows together to make a **9-Patch Block**. Make nine 9-Patch Blocks.

9-Patch Block (make 9)

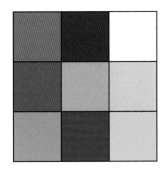

2. Referring to **Diagram A**, cut one 9-Patch Block in half horizontally and vertically following the dashed lines on the diagram. This can be done without moving the block if you have a cutting mat small enough to turn on your work surface.

Diagram A

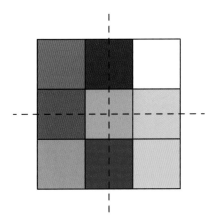

3. Slightly separate the 4 pieces on your mat and turn each piece counter clockwise, one-quarter turn (**Fig. 1**). Keeping pieces in this position, sew 2 top pieces together. Press seam allowances to 1 side. Sew 2 bottom pieces together. Press seam allowances to opposite sides. Matching seams, sew pieces together to make a 4-Patch Block. Press seam allowances to one side.

Fig. 1

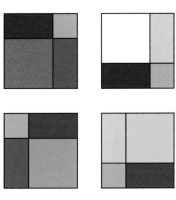

4-Patch Block

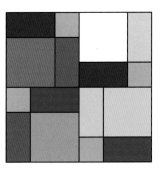

4. Repeat Steps 1-4 to make a *total* of nine 4-Patch Blocks.

ASSEMBLING THE QUILT TOP

1. Lay out all 4-Patch Blocks. Rearrange by moving and turning blocks as desired to change the color pattern. When you are happy with your quilt top, sew three 4-Patch blocks into a **Row**. Make 3 Rows. Press seam allowances on all odd numbered Rows in one direction and seam allowances on even numbered Row in the opposite direction.

Row (make 3)

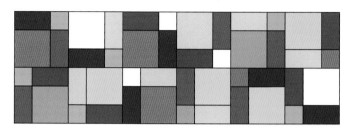

2. Sew Rows together. Due to the fact that there are so many pieces and the blocks may need to be turned to get your desired look, the seam allowances will not always lay in opposite directions. If you wish, you can flip one of the seam allowances as you come to these seams while sewing. Press the seam allowances joining the Rows toward the bottom of the quilt top center.
3. Follow **Adding Squared Borders**, page 86, to add **borders** to quilt top center.

QUILTING AND BINDING

1. Follow **Quilting**, page 86, to mark, layer, and quilt. My quilt is machine quilted with a meandering swirl pattern.
2. Follow **Making Templates**, page 82, to make templates using patterns, pages 32-33.
3. Aligning "hilltop" with raw edge on corner of outer border, place corner scallop template on quilt top; mark along scalloped edge of template. Mark each corner in this manner.
4. Using side scallop template, align "hilltop" with raw edge of outer border and match "valley" on side scallop pattern with "valley" on corner scallop pattern. Matching hilltops and valleys, move side scallop template along outer borders and mark along scalloped edge of template.
5. Follow **Binding Scalloped Edges**, page 95, to bind quilt.

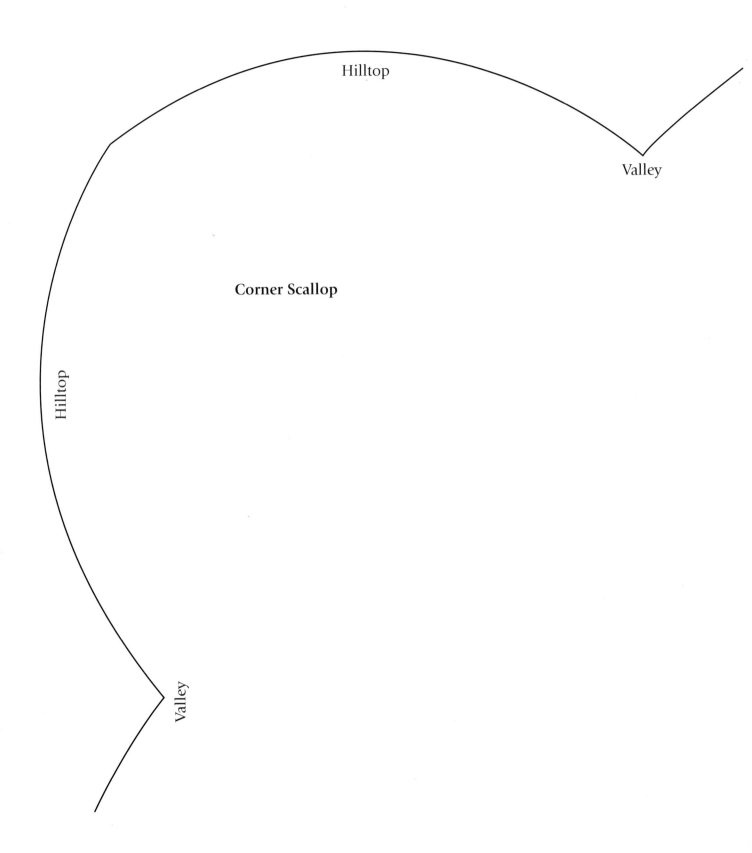

Hilltop

Valley

Hilltop

Corner Scallop

Valley

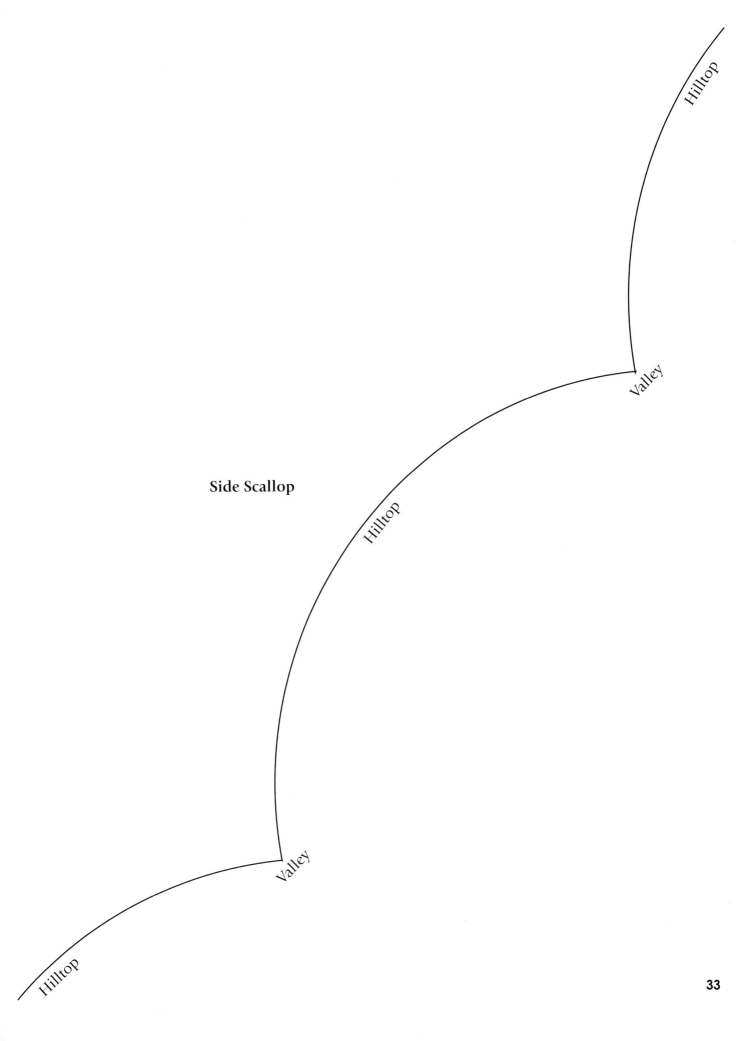

Side Scallop

Sweet Magnolias
quilt

The idea for this quilt came to me after seeing the block "Magnolia Bud" in a book of vintage quilts. I made a few minor changes in the block to make it more beginner friendly and added the scrappy 16-Patch Blocks to soften the overall look of the quilt. To soften the look even more, I added the scalloped edge. The quilt consists of 25 Flower Blocks and twenty-four 16-Patch Blocks. I added a small middle border and the scalloped outside border for a real southern feel.

Finished Quilt Size:
  75" x 75" (191 cm x 191 cm)
Finished Block Size:
  8" x 8" (20 cm x 20 cm)

YARDAGE REQUIREMENTS

Yardage is based on 43"/44" (109 cm/112 cm) wide fabric with a usable width of 40" (102 cm). A fat quarter measures approximately 18" x 22" (46 cm x 56 cm).

Note: Check to make sure your fat quarters measure 18" x 22" (46 cm x 56 cm). If not, buy an extra one to cover your fabric needs.

- 16 assorted light green print fat quarters for the 16-Patch Blocks and Inner Borders
- 1 ivory, 1 peach, and 2 pink print fat quarters for flowers
- 1 raspberry print fat quarter for flower centers
- 3 assorted dark green print fat quarters for leaves
- $^3/_8$ yd (34 cm) of pink print fabric for middle borders
- $1^5/_8$ yds (1.5 m) of ivory print fabric for outer borders
- 7 yds (6.4 m) of fabric for backing
- $^3/_4$ yd (69 cm) of fabric for binding

You will also need:
- 83" x 83" (211 cm x 211 cm) piece of batting

CUTTING THE PIECES

*Follow **Rotary Cutting**, page 82, to cut fabric. Cut all strips across the selvage-to-selvage width of the fabric unless otherwise indicated. Borders include extra length for "insurance" and will be trimmed after assembling quilt top center. All measurements include $^1/_4$" seam allowances.*

From light green print fat quarters:
- Cut a *total* of 48 **strips** $2^1/_2$" x 22" for the 16-Patch Blocks.
- Cut a *total* of 16 **inner border strips** $2^1/_2$" x 22". From 4 of these strips, cut 1 **inner border square** $2^1/_2$" x $2^1/_2$".
- Cut a *total* of 25 strips $2^1/_2$" x 22". From these strips, cut a *total* of 200 **squares** $2^1/_2$" x $2^1/_2$" for the Magnolia Blocks.

From ivory, peach, and pink print fat quarters:
- Cut a *total* of 25 sets of 1 **square** $4^1/_2$" x $4^1/_2$" and 2 **rectangles** $2^1/_2$" x $4^1/_2$" for Magnolia Blocks.

From raspberry print fat quarter:
- For *each* of 25 Magnolia Blocks, cut 1 **square** $2^1/_2$" x $2^1/_2$" for flower center.

Continued on page 38.

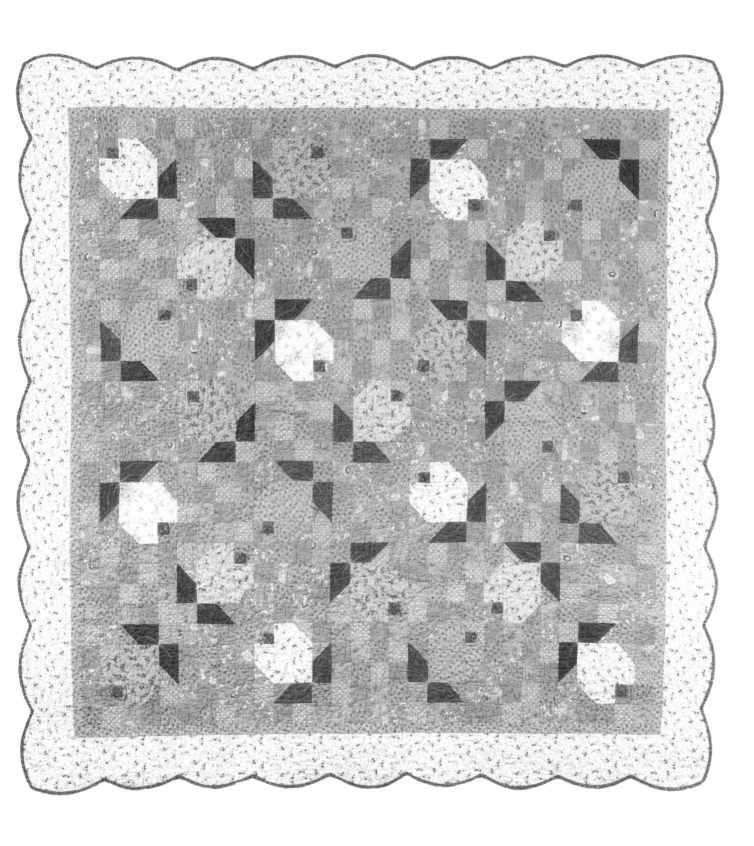

Sweet Magnolias continued.

From dark green print fat quarters:
- Cut a *total* of 13 strips 2$^1/_2$" x 22". From these strips, cut a *total* of 25 sets of 2 matching **rectangles** 2$^1/_2$" x 4$^1/_2$".

From pink print fabric:
- Cut 2 **side middle borders** 1$^1/_2$" x 64$^1/_2$", pieced as needed.
- Cut 2 **top/bottom middle borders** 1$^1/_2$" x 66$^1/_2$", pieced as needed.

From ivory print fabric:
- Cut 2 **side outer borders** 6$^1/_2$" x 66$^1/_2$", pieced as needed.
- Cut 2 **top/bottom outer borders** 6$^1/_2$" x 78$^1/_2$", pieced as needed.

ASSEMBLING THE MAGNOLIA BLOCKS
*Follow **Machine Piecing**, page 84, and **Pressing**, page 85. Use a scant $^1/_4$" seam allowance.*

*If you look closely at the **Magnolia Block Assembly Diagram** you can see that it is actually a fancy version of a 9-Patch Block. When you think of it that way, work on each of the 9 pieces one at a time, then sew them together as you would any 9-Patch, it makes it seem a lot easier. Let's get started.*

1. Choose 2 assorted light green **squares**. Draw a diagonal line across each square.
2. For leaves, match right sides and place 1 light green square on 1 end of each of 2 matching dark green **rectangles** (**Fig. 1**) and stitch along drawn line. Note that the diagonal lines are going in opposite directions. This is a must. This will insure that your leaves are mirror images, which is necessary to make this block.

Fig. 1

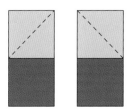

3. Trim $^1/_4$" from stitching line (**Fig. 2**). Open up and press seam allowances toward darker fabric to make two **Unit 1's**. Unit 1's should measure 2$^1/_2$" x 4$^1/_2$".

Fig. 2   **Unit 1** (make 2)

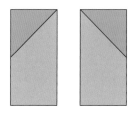

4. For flower, choose 2 matching ivory, peach, or pink **rectangles**. Repeat Steps 1-3 to make two **Unit 2's**. It is still important to make sure these are mirror images.

Unit 2 (make 2)

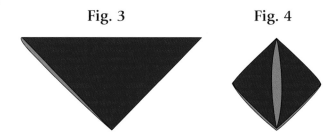

5. For flower center, choose 1 light green square and 1 raspberry square.
6. Matching right sides, fold raspberry square in half (**Fig. 3**). Fold each corner to meet the center point (**Fig. 4**). Press carefully so this lays nice and flat.

Fig. 3   **Fig. 4**

7. Matching the corner and sides, place folded square on the corner of the light green square (**Fig. 5**). All raw edges should be to the outside of the square. Baste a couple of stitches across the center of the folded square to hold it in place while you assemble the block.

Fig. 5

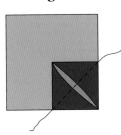

8. Refer to **Magnolia Block Assembly Diagram** to lay out the pieces of your Magnolia Block. Sew the pieces into horizontal Rows. Press the seam allowances on the top and bottom Rows toward the center piece. Press the seam allowances on the middle Row away from the center piece. Matching the seams, sew the Rows together. Press the seam allowances in 1 direction.

9. Repeat Steps 1-8 to make a *total* of 25 Magnolia Blocks.

Magnolia Block Assembly Diagram

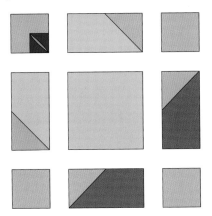

ASSEMBLING THE 16-PATCH BLOCKS

1. Sew 4 light green **strips** together to make **Strip Set A**; press the seam allowances in 1 direction. Make 12 Strip Set A's. The more random these are, the easier it is to keep the scrappy look throughout the quilt. Cut across Strip Set A's at $2^1/_2$" intervals to make 96 **Unit 3's**. Unit 3's should measure $2^1/_2$" x $8^1/_2$".

Strip Set A (make 12) **Unit 3** (make 96)

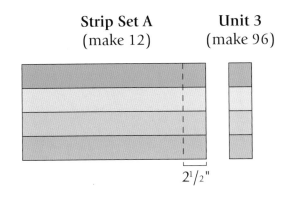

$2^1/_2$"

2. Turning seam allowances in opposite directions and matching seams, sew 4 Unit 4's together to make **16-Patch Block**. Make twenty-four 16-Patch Blocks.

16-Patch Block (make 24)

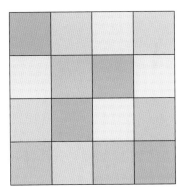

ASSEMBLING THE QUILT TOP

1. Alternating Blocks and turning Blocks as desired, lay out Blocks in Rows of 7 Blocks each. Sew Blocks together into Rows. Press seam allowances toward the Magnolia Blocks.

2. Matching seams, sew Rows together to make quilt top center. Due to the fact that there are so many pieces and the Blocks may be turned to produce the scrappy effect, not all seams will be going in the opposite direction; press seams to opposite side as needed.

ADDING INNER BORDER

1. Sew 4 light green **inner border strips** together to make **Strip Set B**; press the seam allowances in 1 direction. Make 4 Strip Set B's. Remember the 4 strips you cut a square off the end? Use these 4 together in one Strip Set. Cut across Strip Set B's at $2^1/_2$" intervals to make 28 **Unit 5's**. Unit 5's should measure $2^1/_2$" x $8^1/_2$".

Strip Set B
(make 4)

Unit 5
(make 28)

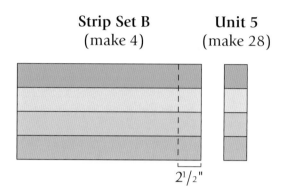

$2^1/_2$"

2. Sew 7 Unit 5's together in random order to make 1 **Inner Border**. Make 4 Inner Borders.

Inner Border (make 4)

3. Matching seams, sew 2 Inner Borders to each side of quilt top center.
4. Sew 1 green **inner border square** to each end of each remaining Inner Border. Sew 1 Inner Border to top and bottom of quilt top center.

ADDING MIDDLE AND OUTER BORDERS

1. Follow **Adding Squared Borders**, page 86, to add **side**, then **top** and **bottom middle borders**. Press seam allowances toward the borders.
2. Add **outer borders** in the same manner. Press seam allowances toward the borders.

QUILTING AND BINDING

1. Follow **Quilting**, page 86, to mark, layer, and quilt. My quilt is machine quilted with 3 "petals" in the flower of the Magnolia Blocks, leaves in each leaf of the Magnolia Blocks, and an all-over meandering leaf pattern over the remainder of the quilt.
2. Follow **Making Templates**, page 82, to make templates using patterns, page 41.
3. Aligning "hilltops" with raw edge on corner of outer border, place corner scallop template on quilt top; mark along scalloped edge of template. Mark each corner in this manner.
4. Using side scallop template, align "hilltop" with raw edge of outer border and match "valley" on side scallop pattern with "valley" on corner scallop pattern. Matching hilltops and valleys, move side scallop template along outer borders and mark along scalloped edge of template.
5. Cut a 22" x 22" square from fabric for binding. Follow **Making Continuous Bias Strip Binding**, page 90, Steps 1-7, to make 320" of $1^1/_4$"w bias binding. Follow **Binding Scalloped Edges**, page 95, to bind quilt.

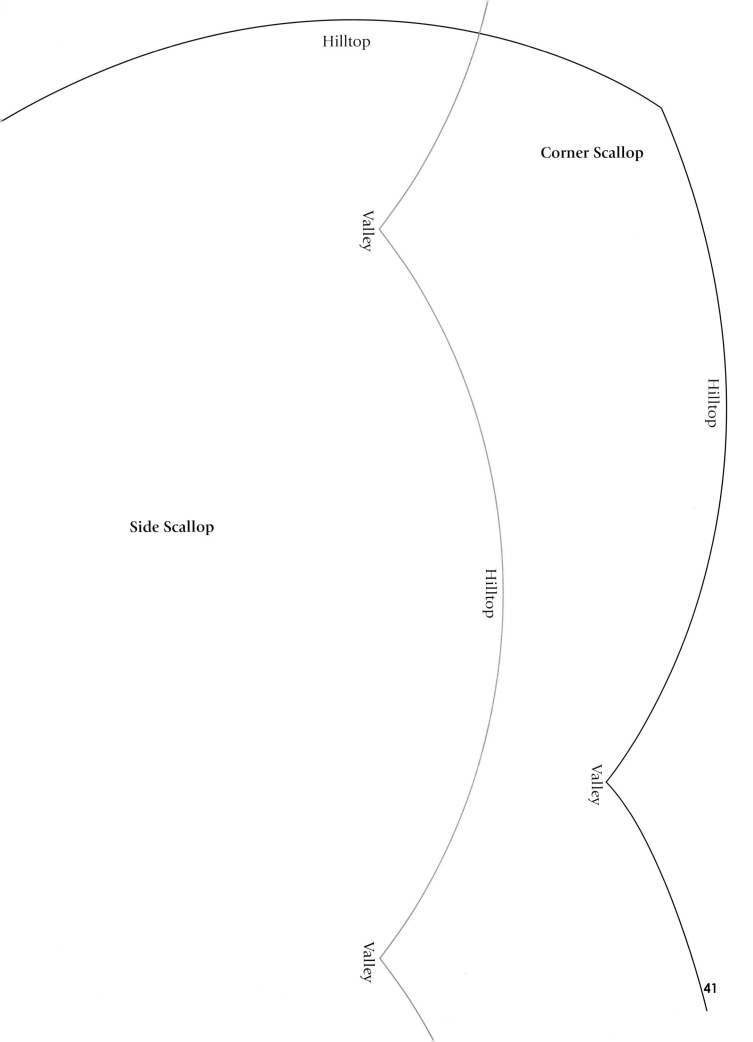

Hilltop

Corner Scallop

Valley

Hilltop

Side Scallop

Hilltop

Valley

Valley

100% Cotton
quilt

This is a jelly-roll friendly pattern. What is a jelly roll you ask? A jelly roll is 40 pre-cut $2^1/_2$" x 42" strips, all from the same fabric collection. They are rolled up and tied to look like a bakery-fresh jelly roll. I think you will really enjoy the ease of using these strips in making your quilt.

Finished Quilt Size:
  61" x 85" (155 cm x 216 cm)
Finished Block Size:
  12" x 12" (30 cm x 30 cm)

YARDAGE REQUIREMENTS

Yardage is based on 43"/44" (109 cm/112 cm) wide fabric with a usable width of 40" (102 cm). A fat quarter measures approximately 18" x 22" (46 cm x 56 cm).

- 1 jelly roll - Choose 24 dark strips for the "thread" on the spools. Any remaining brown strips can be used for "spool ends." Any remaining light strips can be used as "background."
- 6 brown small print or solid fat quarters for the wooden "spool ends." *(Note: For every four strips of browns used from the jelly roll, delete one fat quarter.)*
- 6 light small print or solid fat quarters for the "background." *(Note: It is up to you whether each background piece is cut from the same fabric or different fabrics for a scrappy look. For every four strips of lights used from the jelly roll, delete one fat quarter.)*
- $2^{1}/_{8}$ yds (1.9 m) of print fabric for border
- $5^{1}/_{4}$ yds (4.8 m) of fabric for backing
- $^{3}/_{4}$ yd (69 cm) of fabric for binding

You will also need:

- 69" x 93" (175 cm x 236 cm) piece of batting

CUTTING THE PIECES

*Follow **Rotary Cutting**, page 82, to cut fabric. Borders include extra length for "insurance" and will be trimmed after assembling quilt top center. All measurements include $^{1}/_{4}$" seam allowances.*

From 24 dark print strips chosen from jelly rolls:
- Cut each strip in half to make 48 **"thread" strips**.

From brown small print or solid jelly roll strips and fat quarters:
- From *each* jelly roll strip, cut a set of 2 **rectangles** $2^{1}/_{2}$" x $8^{1}/_{2}$" and 4 **squares** $2^{1}/_{2}$" x $2^{1}/_{2}$". You will need one set of these "spool end" pieces for each Spool Block. I suggest that as you cut each set, you pin them together.
- From fat quarters, refer to **Cutting Diagram A**, page 46, to continue to cut sets of 2 **rectangles** $2^{1}/_{2}$" x $8^{1}/_{2}$" and 4 **squares** $2^{1}/_{2}$" x $2^{1}/_{2}$" until you have a *total* of 24 sets. *(Note: Depending on the number of brown strips in your jelly roll, you may not need to cut all of each fat quarter into sets.)*

Continued on page 46.

100% Cotton continued.

From light small print or solid jelly roll strips and fat quarters:

- From *each* jelly roll strip, cut a set of 2 **background rectangles** $2^1/2$" x $12^1/2$". You will need one set of these pieces for each Spool Block. As you cut the pieces, pin 1 set to each "spool end" stack you cut from browns.
- From fat quarters, refer to **Cutting Diagram B** to continue to cut sets of 2 **background rectangles** $2^1/2$" x $12^1/2$" until you have a *total* of 24 sets. *(Note: Depending on the number of light strips in your jelly roll, you may not need to cut all of each fat quarter into sets.)*

From fabric for border:

- Cut 2 *lengthwise* **side borders** $6^1/2$" x $76^1/2$".
- Cut 2 *lengthwise* **top/bottom borders** $6^1/2$" x $64^1/2$".

Cutting Diagram A

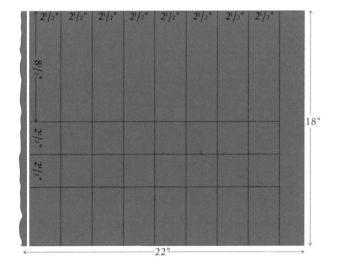

ASSEMBLING THE SPOOL BLOCKS

*Follow **Machine Piecing**, page 84, and **Pressing**, page 85. Use a scant $^1/4$" seam allowance.*

1. *(Note: Keep all the selvage edges at the same end to avoid waste. Your "thread" strips can be all the same general color or you can mix them up for a variegated look. I did a little of both on my quilt.)* Sew 4 dark print **"thread" strips** together to make **Strip Set A**; press the seam allowances in 1 direction. Make 12 Strip Set A's. Cut across Strip Set A's at $8^1/2$" intervals to make **Unit 1**. Make 24 Unit 1's. Unit 1's should measure $8^1/2$" x $8^1/2$".

Strip Set A (make 12)   **Unit 1** (make 24)

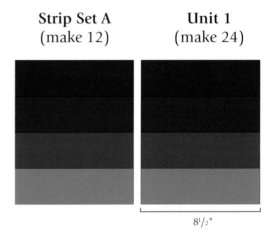

Cutting Diagram B

2. Choose 1 Unit 1 and 1 set of **spool ends** and **background rectangles** you have pinned together. Sew 1 brown **rectangle** to each end of Unit 1 (**Fig. 1**). Press the seam allowances toward the "thread" strips.

Fig. 1

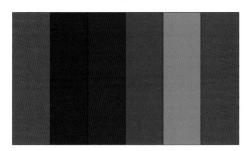

3. Draw a diagonal line on wrong side of each brown **square**. Making sure the two drawn lines are going in opposite directions, sew 1 brown square to each end of 1 light **background rectangle** along the drawn line (**Fig. 2**).

Fig. 2

4. Trim ¹/₄" from stitching line (**Fig. 3**). Open up and press seam allowances toward darker fabric to make **Unit 2**.

Fig. 3

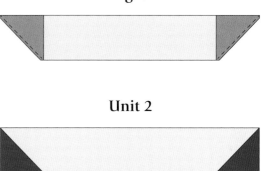

Unit 2

5. Sew 1 Unit 2 to each side of Unit 1 to make **Spool Block**. Make 24 Spool Blocks.
6. Repeat Steps 2-5 to make 24 Spool Blocks.

Spool Block (make 24)

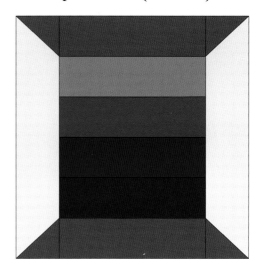

ASSEMBLING THE QUILT TOP

1. Referring to **Quilt Top Diagram**, page 45, and rotating every other Block, lay out **Spool Blocks** in 6 Rows of 4 Blocks each. Press seam allowances on all odd numbered rows in one direction and seam allowances on all even numbered rows in the opposite direction.
2. Sew the Rows together, pressing the seam allowances joining the Rows toward the bottom of the quilt top.

ADDING BORDERS

1. Follow **Adding Squared Borders**, page 86, to add **side**, then **top** and **bottom borders**. Press seam allowances toward the borders.

QUILTING AND BINDING

1. Follow **Quilting**, page 86, to mark, layer, and quilt. My quilt is machine quilted with meandering loops in the background of each block and border and horizontal lines representing thread in each spool. A few of the blocks have a quilted "thread tail".

2. Follow **Making Templates**, page 82, to make templates using pattern, page 49.
3. Referring to arrows on **Quilt Top Diagram**, draw an "imaginary" line from the seamlines between blocks to the edge of the borders; mark each point at edge of borders.
4. Beginning at corner and working toward center of each border and using scallop template, align point of "valley" with each mark on border. Mark along "valley" of scallop template.
5. Trim quilt top along drawn lines.
6. Cut a 22" x 22" square from fabric for binding. Follow **Making Continuous Bias Strip Binding**, page 90, Steps 1-7, to make 320" of $1^1/_4$"w bias binding. Follow **Binding Scalloped Edges**, page 95, to bind quilt.

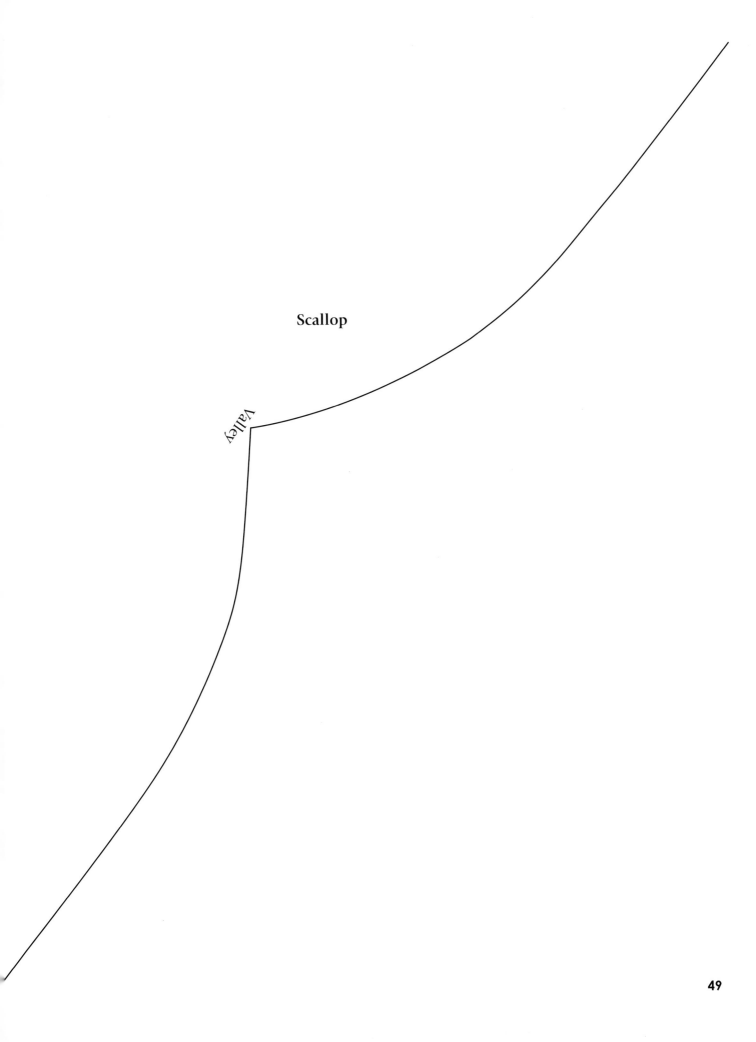

Scallop

Valley

Indian Summer
quilt

This small quilt looks more difficult than it really is. The pattern is made up of mostly strip sets and a few larger pieces cut from your background fabric. It goes together in no time and with little effort. Try a light background for a completely different look.

Finished Quilt Size:
   53¹/₂" x 53¹/₂" (136 cm x 136 cm)
Finished Block Size:
   9" x 9" (23 cm x 23 cm)

YARDAGE REQUIREMENTS

Yardage is based on 43"/44" (109 cm/112 cm) wide fabric with a usable width of 40" (102 cm) for cotton fabrics. A fat quarter measures approximately 18" x 22" (46 cm x 56 cm).

> 2³/₄ yds (2.5 m) of black print fabric for background and border
>
> 8 assorted fat quarters **OR** a *total* of 32 strips 2" x 22" (5 cm x 56 cm) from at least 8 different colors
>
> 3¹/₂ yds (3.2 m) of fabric for backing
>
> ⁵/₈ yd (57 cm) of fabric for binding

You will also need:

> 62" x 62" (157 cm x 157 cm) piece of batting

CUTTING THE PIECES

*Follow **Rotary Cutting**, page 82, to cut fabric. Cut all strips across the selvage-to-selvage width of the fabric. Borders include extra length for "insurance" and will be trimmed after assembling quilt top center. All measurements include ¹/₄" seam allowances.*

A Tip from *Cardiff Farm:*

If you are going to be moving this project from one place to another, try using plastic bags to keep all your pieces straight. Label your bags A through H and as you cut your pieces or cut segments, put them into the appropriate bag. This will also prevent the edges from becoming frayed or distorted. If you are able to sew your entire project in one place, you can label your stacks with sticky notes.

From black print fabric for background and border:

- Cut 16 strips 2"w. Cut each strip in half to make 32 **strips** 2" x 20".
- Cut 2 strips 3¹/₂"w. From these strips, cut 4 squares 3¹/₂" x 3¹/₂" (**A**) and 12 rectangles 3¹/₂" x 5" (**B**).
- Cut 2 strips 5"w. From these strips, cut 12 rectangles 5" x 6¹/₂" (**C**).
- Cut 2 **side borders** 6¹/₂" x 45", pieced as needed.
- Cut 2 **top/bottom borders** 6¹/₂" x 57", pieced as needed.

From assorted fat quarters:

- Cut a *total* of 32 **strips** 2" x 22".

Continued on page 54.

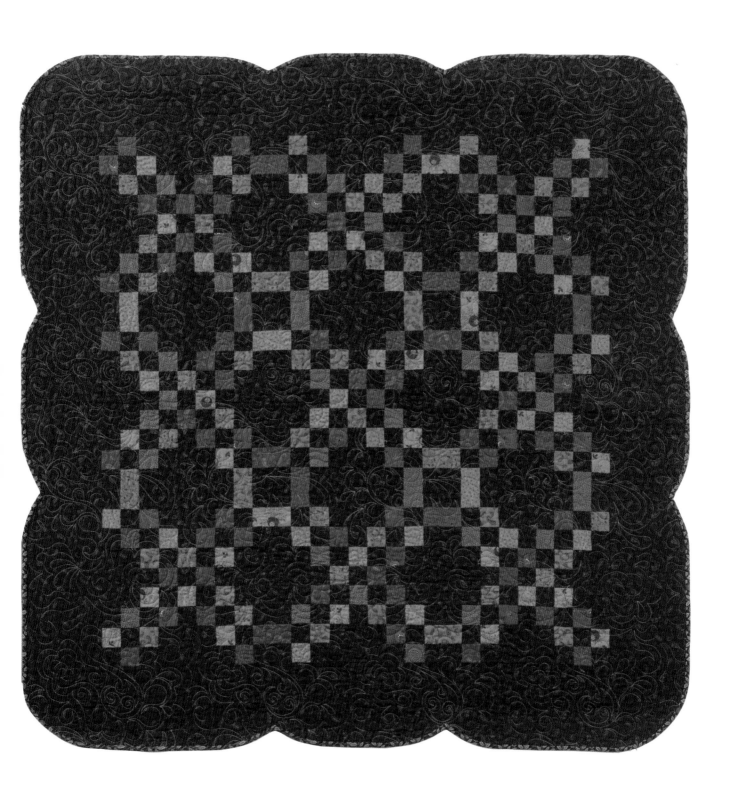

Indian Summer continued.

ASSEMBLING THE BLOCKS
Follow **Machine Piecing**, *page 84, and* **Pressing**, *page 85. Use a scant* $^1/_4$" *seam allowance.*

Follow **Machine Piecing**, *page 84, and* **Pressing**, *page 85.*

1. Sew 1 black print strip and 1 colored print strip together to make **Strip Set A**; press the seam allowances toward the colored fabric. Make 24 Strip Set A's. Set aside 16 Strip Set A's. From **each** remaining Strip Set A, cut 2 segments at $3^1/_2$" intervals to make 16 **D's**.

Strip Set A
(make 24)

D
(make 2 from each of 8 Strip Set A's)

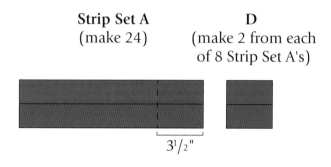

$3^1/_2$"

2. Still working with the same 8 Strip Set A's, cut 4 segments from each at 2" intervals to make 32 **E's**.

E (make 32)

3. Working with 8 of the Strip Set A's set aside previously, sew a black print strip to the side of the colored strip on each set to make **Strip Set B**. Make 8 Strip Set B's. Press the seam allowances toward the colored fabric.

Strip Set B (make 8)

4. From **each** Strip Set B, cut one segment at a $3^1/_2$" interval to make 8 **F's**. From Strip Set B's, also cut a *total* of 42 segments at 2" intervals to make 42 **G's**.

F (make 8)

G (make 42)

5. Working with the 8 remaining Strip Set A's set aside previously, sew a colored print strip (different than the color already in the Strip Set) to the side of the black print strip on each set to make **Strip Set C**. Make 8 Strip Set C's. Press the seam allowances toward the colored fabric.

Strip Set C (make 8)

6. From each Strip Set C, cut segments at 2" intervals to make a *total* of 65 **H's**.

H (make 65)

7. Sew 2 piece G's and 1 piece H together to make a **9-Patch Block**. Press seam allowances toward center row. Make 13 9-Patch Blocks.

9-Patch Block (make 13)

8. Sew 1 piece H and 1 piece B together to make **Unit 1**. Press seam allowances toward H. Make 12 Unit 1's.

Unit 1 (make 12)

9. Sew 2 pieces H and 1 piece C together to make **Unit 2**. Press seam allowances toward H's. Make 12 Unit 2's.

Unit 2 (make 12)

10. Sew 1 piece F, 2 pieces G, and 2 pieces H together to make **Unit 3**. Press seam allowances toward H's. Make 8 Unit 3's.

Unit 3 (make 8)

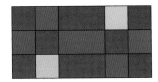

11. Sew 2 piece E's together to make a **4-Patch Block**. Press seam allowances either direction. Make 16 4-Patch Blocks.

4-Patch Block (make 16)

12. Sew 4 4-Patch Blocks, 4 piece D's, and 1 piece A together to make **Block**. Make 4 Blocks.

Block (make 4)

ASSEMBLING THE QUILT TOP
1. Refer to **Assembly Diagram**, page 56, lay out Units and Blocks. Arrange so that colors are scattered.
2. Sew Units and Blocks into horizontal rows. Press seam allowances toward the pieces containing B's or C's (the largest background pieces cut). Sew the Rows together, pressing the seam allowances joining the Rows toward the bottom of the quilt top center.

ADDING BORDERS
1. Follow **Adding Squared Borders**, page 86, to add **side**, then **top** and **bottom borders**. Press seam allowances toward the borders.

QUILTING AND BINDING

1. Follow **Quilting**, page 86, to mark, layer, and quilt. My quilt is machine quilted with an overall swirl pattern.
2. Follow **Making Templates**, page 82, to make templates using pattern, page 57.
3. To round corners of quilt top, draw an "imaginary" line from the corner of the quilt top center to the corner of the quilt top. To mark half of corner, use template and align point of valley with imaginary line and straight edge of template with straight edge of quilt top. Mark from point of valley along straight edge. Reverse template and mark remaining half of corner. Mark remaining corners in same manner.
4. Referring to dashed lines on **Assembly Diagram**, draw an "imaginary" line from the center of each outer Unit 3 to the edge of the borders; mark each "valley" at edge of borders. Align point of "valley" with each mark on border. Mark along "valley" of template.
5. Trim quilt top along drawn lines.
6. Cut a 20" x 20" square from fabric for binding. Follow **Making Continuous Bias Strip Binding**, page 90, Steps 1-7, to make 240" of 1¹/₄"w bias binding. Follow **Binding Scalloped Edges**, page 95, to bind quilt.

Assembly Diagram

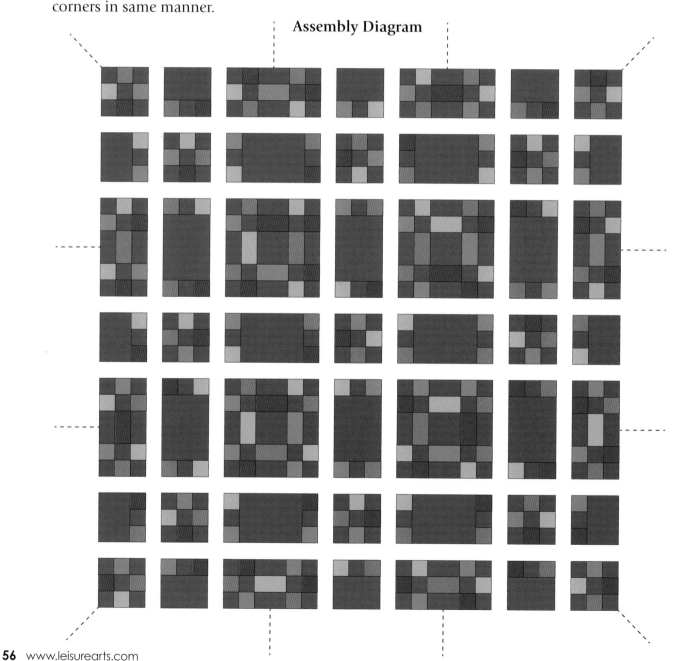

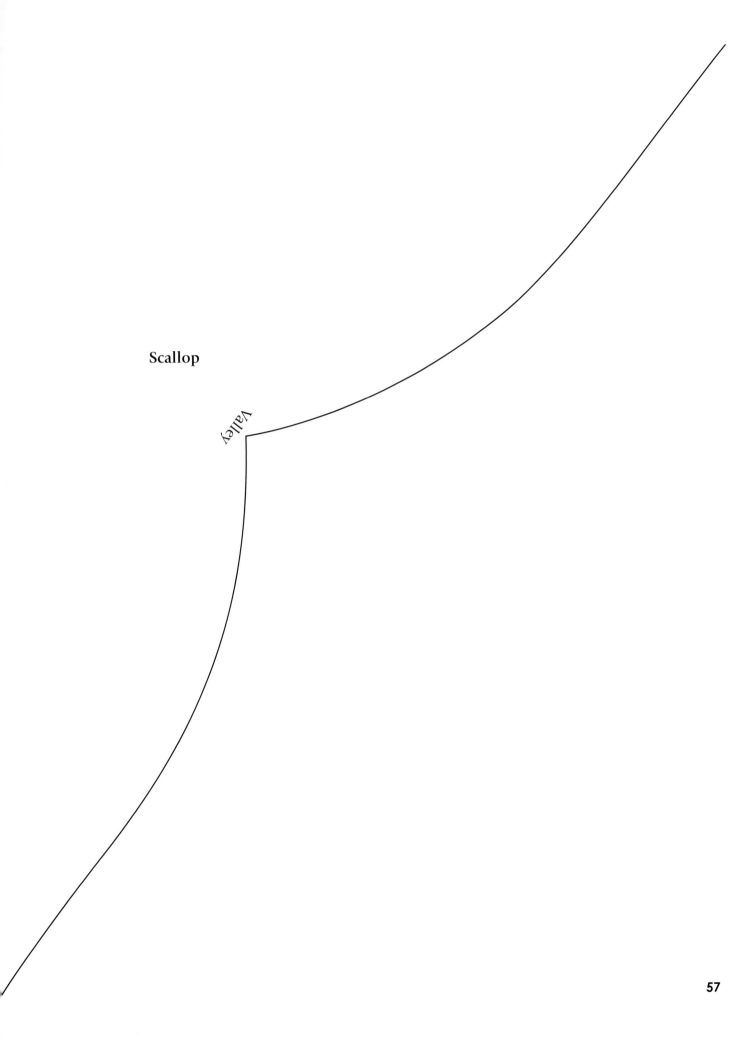

Scallop

Valley

Reflections
quilt

This quilt was made from leftovers of my past quilts. My daughter and I had a wonderful time selecting the colors and pairing up the many color combinations. I'm glad I kept all those scraps!

Finished Quilt Size:
65" x 81" (165 cm x 206 cm)
Finished Block Size:
8" x 8" (20 cm x 20 cm)

Eighty 8" x 8" (20 cm x 20 cm) Blocks complete this quilt. Each Block contains 2 pinwheel squares and 2 triangle-squares made from 1 dark fabric and 1 light fabric.

YARDAGE REQUIREMENTS

Yardage is based on 43"/44" (109 cm/112 cm) wide fabric with a usable width of 40" (102 cm). A fat quarter measures approximately 18" x 22" (46 cm x 56 cm).

9 assorted light print fat quarters **OR** 2 matching light print squares 6" x 6" (15 cm x 15 cm) for each of 40 Blocks - white, ivory, and light beige

9 assorted medium print fat quarters **OR** 2 matching medium print squares 6" x 6" (15 cm x 15 cm) for each of 40 Blocks - dark beige, tan, and light brown

18 assorted dark print fat quarters **OR** 2 matching dark print squares 6" x 6" (15 cm x 15 cm) for each of 80 Blocks

5 yds (4.6 m) of fabric for backing

⁷/₈ yd (80 cm) of fabric for binding

You will also need:

73" x 89" (185 cm x 226 cm) piece of batting
Triangles On A Roll™ Half Square Triangles
4" (10 cm) and 2" (5 cm) finished size

CUTTING THE PIECES

*Follow **Rotary Cutting**, page 82, to cut fabric. All measurements include ¹/₄" seam allowances.*

From assorted light print fat quarters:

- For *each* of 40 Blocks, cut 2 matching **squares** 6" x 6".

From assorted medium print fat quarters:

- For *each* of 40 Blocks, cut 2 matching **squares** 6" x 6".

From assorted dark print fat quarters:

- For *each* of 80 Blocks, cut 2 matching **squares** 6" x 6".

MAKING THE TRIANGLE-SQUARES

1. Using 4" finished Triangles On A Roll, cut 80 paper squares. Each square will yield 2 Triangle-Squares, which is enough for 1 Block.

2. Matching right sides and aligning raw edges, place 1 light or medium print and 1 dark print 6" x 6" square together.

3. With dark square on bottom, center one paper square, right side up, on top of the fabric squares; pin in place.

Continued on page 62.

Reflections continued.

4. Adjust your sewing machine stitch length to approximately 20 stitches to the inch. Following the arrows, sew on all dashed lines.

5. Trim paper and excess fabric away on the solid lines around the outside of the square. Cut on the solid diagonal line between the stitching lines.

6. Place triangles, paper side down, on the pressing surface. Give one quick press to set the seam. Lift the corner of the darker fabric with your finger and using the iron to help open, press the square flat to make a **Large Triangle Square**. Make 2 Large Triangle-Squares. This method will press the seam allowance toward the dark fabric. The paper helps to keep the square from stretching out of shape.

7. Remove the paper. For this, I like to grab the paper with both hands and give it a tear from the outside corner toward the seam. Repeat for the remaining outside corner. Now tear away the paper in the seam allowance, grabbing it in the middle and gently pulling.

8. Repeat Steps 2-7 to make 2 matching Large Triangle-Squares for each of 80 Blocks.

Large Triangle Square
(make 2 matching for each of 80 Blocks)

MAKING THE PINWHEEL SQUARES

1. Using 2" finished Triangles On A Roll, cut 4 joined paper squares (**Fig. 1**) for each of the 80 Blocks. These squares will yield 8 Triangle-Squares. This will make 2 Pinwheel Squares, which is enough for 1 Block.

Fig. 1

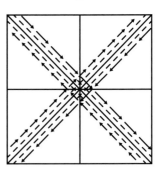

2. Matching right sides and aligning raw edges, place 1 light or medium print and 1 dark print 6" x 6" square together.

3. Repeat **Making the Triangle-Squares**, Steps 3-7, to make 8 Small Triangle-Squares for each of 80 Blocks.

4. Sew 4 matching Small Triangle-Squares together to make **Pinwheel Square**. Press seam allowances toward the dark fabric. Make 2 matching Pinwheel Squares for each of 80 Blocks.

Pinwheel Square
(make 2 matching for each of 80 Blocks)

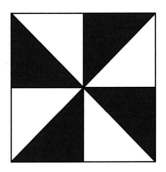

5. Sew 2 matching Large Triangle-Squares and 2 Pinwheel Squares together to make **Block**. Make 80 Blocks.

Block (make 80)

ASSEMBLING THE QUILT TOP

Follow Machine Piecing, page 84, and Pressing, page 85. Use a scant $^1/_4$" seam allowance.

1. Lay out the Blocks into 10 Rows of 8 Blocks each.
2. Sew the Blocks together to make Rows, pressing seam allowances on all odd numbered Rows in one direction and seam allowances on all even numbered Rows in the opposite direction.
3. Sew the Rows together, pressing the seam allowances joining the Rows toward the bottom of the quilt top.

QUILTING AND BINDING

1. Follow **Quilting**, page 86, to mark, layer, and quilt. My quilt is machine quilted with an all-over scallop pattern.
2. Cut a 30" x 30" square of fabric for binding. Follow **Making Continuous Bias Strip Binding**, page 90, to make 300" of $2^1/_2$"w bias binding. Follow **Attaching Binding with Mitered Corners**, page 92, to attach binding to quilt.

Golden Rule quilt

I loved looking through my stash for all the different reds. You can use as many as you like. There are 18 School House Blocks and I used 18 reds. I also used a piece of each red in my binding.

Finished Quilt Size:
71" x 87" (180 cm x 221 cm)
Finished Block Size:
8" x 8" (20 cm x 20 cm)

This quilt is made up of 2 very traditional blocks – the School House Block and the Hourglass Block. The Blocks are simple and go together quickly.

The School House Blocks are made up of 4 sections. A, B, and D are traditionally pieced. Section C is the roof and foundation paper piecing makes the angles easier. On my quilt there is one house pointing the opposite direction. That was my goof for this quilt. I like to leave my goofs in just to remind me not to stress over the little things that don't go just right. If you want one of your houses going the opposite direction have your copy center make you an additional copy with a mirror image.

The Hourglass Blocks, which are made in 3 different shades - light, medium, and dark, fill in the background and create a secondary pattern.

YARDAGE REQUIREMENTS

Yardage is based on 43"/44" (109 cm/112 cm) wide fabric with a usable width of 40" (102 cm). A fat quarter measures approximately 18" x 22" (46 cm x 56 cm). A fat eighth measures approximately 9" x 22" (23 cm x 56 cm).

- 6 assorted beige/light tan print fat quarters for background
- 13 assorted tan/light gold print fat quarters for background
- 4 assorted dark gold print fat quarters for background
- 7 assorted black print fat eighths for doors and windows
- 12 assorted brown/black print fat quarters for roofs
- 18 assorted red print fat eighths for school houses and binding
- $3/8$ yd (34 cm) of red print for inner border
- $7/8$ yd (80 cm) **each** of 2 different black prints for outer border
- $5 3/8$ yds (4.9 m) of fabric for backing

You will also need:
- 79" x 95" (201 cm x 241 cm) piece of batting

Continued on page 68.

Golden Rule continued.

CUTTING THE PIECES
Follow Rotary Cutting, page 82, to cut fabric. Cut all strips across the selvage-to-selvage width of the fabric unless otherwise indicated. Borders include extra length for "insurance" and will be trimmed after assembling quilt top center. All measurements include $^1/_4$" seam allowances.

From the light and medium print fabrics, you will be cutting for the Hourglass Blocks as well as the background for the School Houses. From the dark gold fabrics, you will be cutting for the Hourglass Blocks only. I kept my colors separated in stacks because the backgrounds of each School House Block are the same. But if you are making them scrappy, just stack like sizes together so you don't have to measure them again while sewing.

From each beige/light tan print fat quarter (lights):
- Cut 2 **large squares** 10" x 10" for a *total* of 12 for the Hourglass Blocks.
- From the remainder of *each* fat quarter, cut the following for the School House Blocks:
  - 2 squares $3^1/_2$" x $3^1/_2$". Cut each square once diagonally to make 24 **triangles** for areas #2 and #4 of Section C.
  - 2 **small rectangles** $1^1/_2$" x $3^1/_2$".
  - 4 **very small rectangles** $1^1/_2$" x 2".

From each tan/light gold print fat quarter (mediums):
- Cut 2 **large squares** 10" x 10" for a *total* of 26 for the Hourglass Blocks.
- From the remainder of each of 6 fat quarters, cut the following for the School House Blocks:
  - 1 square $3^1/_2$" x $3^1/_2$". Cut each square once diagonally to make 12 **triangles** for areas #2 and #4 of Section C.
  - 1 **small rectangle** $1^1/_2$" x $3^1/_2$".
  - 2 **very small rectangles** $1^1/_2$" x 2".

From *each* dark gold print fat quarter (darks):
- Cut 2 **large squares** 10" x 10" for a *total* of 8 for the Hourglass Blocks.

From black print fat eighths:
- Cut a *total* of 18 **medium rectangles** $1^1/_2$" x $4^1/_2$" for School House Blocks.
- Cut a *total* of 18 sets of 2 **small rectangles** $1^1/_2$" x $3^1/_2$" for School House Blocks.

From brown/black print fat quarters:
- Cut a *total* of 18 **very large rectangles** $3^1/_2$" x $7^1/_2$" for area #1 of Section C for School House Blocks .

From *each* red print fat eighth:
- Cut 1 **binding strip** $2^1/_2$" x 22".
- From the remainder of *each* fat eighth, cut the following for the School House Blocks:
  - 1 **medium square** 4" x 4" for area #3 of Section C for School House Blocks.
  - 2 **large rectangles** $1^1/_2$" x $5^1/_2$".
  - Cut 2 **medium rectangles** $1^1/_2$" x $4^1/_2$".
  - Cut 4 **small rectangles** $1^1/_2$" x $3^1/_2$".
  - Cut 2 **small squares** $1^1/_2$" x $1^1/_2$".

From red print fabric for inner border:
- Cut 2 **side inner borders** $1^1/_2$" x $76^1/_2$", pieced as needed.
- Cut 2 **top/bottom inner borders** $1^1/_2$" x $62^1/_2$", pieced as needed.

From *each* black print for outer borders:
- Cut 1 **side outer border** $6^1/_2$" x $78^1/_2$", pieced as needed.
- Cut 1 **top/bottom outer border** $6^1/_2$" x $74^1/_2$", pieced as needed.

MAKING SECTION C'S

1. Make 18 copies of the Section C pattern, page 73. Notice that the pattern is reversed so that after you have sewn the sections, they come out pointing in the correct direction. Trim roughly around the pattern leaving a little extra paper outside the dashed line.
2. Shorten the stitch length on your machine to 20 stitches per inch.
3. Lay 1 **very large rectangle** right side up over area #1 on the unprinted side of the paper foundation. If necessary, turn the foundation and paper over and hold them up to a light source or sunlit window to see the placement area. The fabric should completely cover area #1. Pin the rectangle to the foundation or use a dab of fabric glue to hold the rectangle in place.
4. Matching right sides and having at least $1/4$" of the fabric extending into area #2, lay 1 beige/light tan **triangle** over the end of the very large rectangle; pin in place.

5. Turn the paper foundation over so the printed side is now facing up. You will be sewing on the solid line between areas #1 and #2. Start sewing 3 or 4 stitches before the beginning of the line. Stitch on the lines, extending stitching 3 or 4 stitches beyond the end of the line.
6. Fold triangle back over the seam with the right sides facing up, to be sure it covers the entire area #2. Unfold and trim the seam allowances to $1/4$". Refold triangle and press in place.
7. Repeat Steps 4-6 to add remaining pieces in the same manner to complete Section C.
8. When you have sewn all the pieces of Section C together, trim on the dashed line before removing the paper.
9. Repeat Steps 3-8 to make a *total* of 12 Section C's using beige/light tan triangles. Make 6 Section C's using tan/light gold triangles.

MAKING THE SCHOOL HOUSE BLOCKS
*Follow **Machine Piecing**, page 84, and **Pressing**, page 85. Use a scant $1/4$" seam allowance. Press seam allowances toward the darker fabric unless otherwise noted.*

1. Sew 1 red **medium rectangle** to each side of 1 black **medium rectangle**. Press seam allowances toward the black medium rectangle. Sew 1 red **small rectangle** to 1 end to make **Section A**. Press seam allowances toward the small rectangle.

Section A

2. Sew 3 red small rectangles and 2 black **small rectangles** together. Sew a red **large rectangle** to the top and bottom to make **Section B**. Press the seam allowances toward the small rectangles.

Section B

3. Sew 1 beige/light tan **small rectangle**, 2 red **small squares**, and 2 beige/light tan **very small rectangles** together to make **Section D**. Press seam allowances toward beige/light tan rectangles.

Section D

4. Sew Sections A-D together to make **School House Block**. Make 12 School House Block A's.

School House Block A
(make 12)

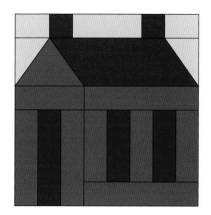

5. Repeat Steps 1-4 substituting tan/light gold pieces for all beige/light tan pieces to make **School House Block B**. Make 6 School House Block B's.

School House Block B
(make 6)

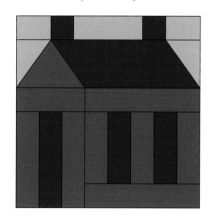

MAKING THE HOURGLASS BLOCKS
Making Triangle-Squares
Pair the **large squares** as follows:
- Make 3 pairs of medium and medium (squares #1).
- Make 12 pairs of medium and light (squares #2).
- Make 8 pairs of medium and dark (squares #3).

1. For each pair of squares, draw a diagonal line on the wrong side of the lighter fabric square.
2. Matching right sides, place 1 marked square on top of 1 unmarked square. Stitch $^1/_4$" from each side of drawn line (**Fig. 1**). Cut along drawn line and press seam allowances to darker fabric to make 2 **Triangle-Squares**. Triangle-Square should measure $9^5/_8$" x $9^5/_8$" including seam allowances. Make 2 Triangle-Squares from each pair of squares (above).

Fig. 1

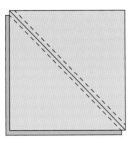

Triangle-Square

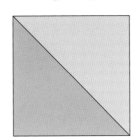

Making Hourglass Block A's
1. Use 4 of the #3 (medium/dark) triangle-squares. On wrong side of 1 Triangle-Square, draw a diagonal line (corner to corner and perpendicular to seam).

2. Matching right sides and seams and with medium fabric facing dark fabric, place marked Triangle-Square on top of unmarked Triangle-Square. Stitch $^1/_4$" from each side of drawn line. Cut apart along drawn line to make 2 **Hourglass Block A's**; press seam allowances to one side. Trim Block to $8^1/_2$" x $8^1/_2$". Make 4 Hourglass Block A's.

Hourglass Block A
(make 4)

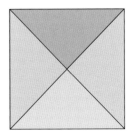

Making Hourglass Block B's
1. Use 7 of the #3 (medium/dark) squares and 7 of the #2 (medium/light) squares and follow Steps 1-2, above, to make **Hourglass Block B**. Make 14 Hourglass Block B's.

Hourglass Block B
(make 14)

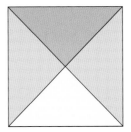

Making Hourglass Block C's

1. Use 5 of the #1 (medium/medium) squares and 5 of the #3 (medium/dark) squares to make **Hourglass Block C** in the same manner. Make 10 Hourglass Block C's. You will have 1 (medium/medium) Triangle-Square left over; discard.

Hourglass Block C
(make 10)

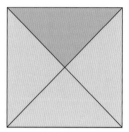

Making Hourglass Block D's

1. Use 16 of the #2 (medium/light) squares to make **Hourglass Block D** in the same manner. Make 16 Hourglass Block D's.

Note: To make the last Hourglass D, take the last #2 (medium/light) square and cut on the diagonal where you would otherwise be drawing the line. Unsew the seam on one half. Switch the position of the medium and light fabrics and resew. Place right sides together with the other half and sew with a $1/4$" seam allowance to make Hourglass D.

Hourglass Block D
(make 17)

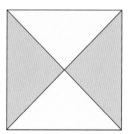

ASSEMBLING THE QUILT TOP

1. Lay out the Blocks in 9 Rows of 7 Blocks each.
2. Sew the Blocks together to make Rows, pressing seam allowances on all odd numbered Rows in one direction and seam allowances on all even numbered Rows in the opposite direction.
3. Sew the Rows together, pressing the seam allowances joining the Rows towards the bottom of the quilt top.
4. Follow **Adding Squared Borders**, page 86, to add **side**, then **top** and **bottom inner borders** to quilt top center.
5. Add **outer borders** to quilt top in same manner.

QUILTING AND BINDING

1. Follow **Quilting**, page 86, to mark, layer, and quilt. My quilt is machine quilted with meandering swirls.
2. Cut a 31" x 31" square of fabric for binding. Follow **Making Continuous Bias Strip Binding**, page 90, to make $2^1/2$"w bias binding. Follow **Attaching Binding with Mitered Corners**, page 92, to attach binding to quilt.

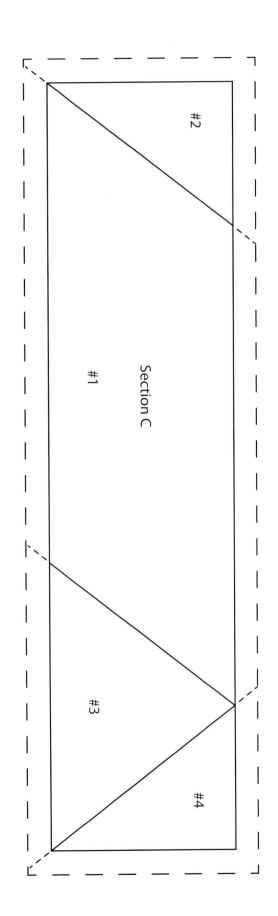

Leisure Arts, Inc. grants permission to the owner of this publication to copy this pattern for personal use only.

Farmer's Market
quilt

This quilt was really quick and easy to make. It is made up of 196 triangle-squares, half being a light fabric and half being a darker, contrasting fabric. I used five charm packs but it can easily be made from fat quarters or your stash. As long as you can cut a 5" square on the straight grain it will work. In addition, I added fabrics for borders, backing, and binding. Just relax and have fun picking your colors. Pick as many as you like.

Finished Quilt Size:
71" x 71" (180 cm x 180 cm)

YARDAGE REQUIREMENTS

Yardage is based on 43"/44" (109 cm/112 cm) wide fabric with a usable width of 40" (102 cm). A fat quarter measures approximately 18" x 22" (46 cm x 56 cm) and yields twelve squares 5" x 5" (13 cm x 13 cm) .

> 98 light print 5" x 5" (13 cm x 13 cm) squares and 98 medium to dark print 5" x 5" (13 cm x 13 cm) squares from charm packs. Squares can also be cut from 9 light print fat quarters and 9 medium to dark print fat quarters.
> $^3/_8$ yd (34 m) of dark print fabric for inner border
> $1^1/_2$ yds (1.4 m) of light print fabric for outer border
> $4^1/_2$ yds (4.1 m) of fabric for backing
> $^3/_4$ yd (69 cm) of fabric for binding

You will also need:

> 79" x 79" (201 cm x 201 cm) piece of batting

CUTTING THE PIECES

*Follow **Rotary Cutting**, page 82, to cut fabric. Cut all strips across the selvage-to-selvage width of the fabric. Borders include extra length for "insurance" and will be trimmed after assembling quilt top center. All measurements include $^1/_4$" seam allowances.*

If using fat quarters:
- From *each* fat quarter, cut 3 strips 5" x 22". From these strips, cut a *total* of 98 light print **squares** 5" x 5" and 98 medium to dark print **squares** 5" x 5".

From fabric for inner borders:
- Cut 2 **top/bottom inner borders** $1^1/_2$" x $62^1/_2$", pieced as needed.
- Cut 2 **side inner borders** $1^1/_2$" x $60^1/_2$", pieced as needed.

From fabric for outer borders:
- Cut 2 **top/bottom outer borders** $6^1/_2$" x $74^1/_2$", pieced as needed.
- Cut 2 **side outer borders** $6^1/_2$" x $62^1/_2$", pieced as needed.

Continued on page 78.

MAKING THE TRIANGLE-SQUARES

1. Draw a diagonal line on wrong side of each light print **square**.
2. Matching right sides, place 1 light square on top of 1 medium to dark square. Stitch ¹/₄" from each side of drawn line (**Fig. 1**). Cut along drawn line and press seam allowances toward the dark fabric to make 2 **Triangle-Squares**. Make 196 Triangle-Squares. Trim each Triangle-Square to 4¹/₂" x 4¹/₂".

Fig. 1

Triangle-Square (make 196)

ASSEMBLING THE QUILT TOP

*Follow **Machine Piecing**, page 84, and **Pressing**, page 85. Use a scant ¹/₄" seam allowance.*

1. Refer to **Quarter Section Assembly Diagram**, below, to assemble one quarter section of quilt top center. Take note as to where the dark and light prints are and which direction the diagonal seam is going. Sew the Triangle-Squares into Rows. Press seam allowances on all odd numbered Rows in one direction and seam allowances on all even numbered Rows in the opposite direction. Sew Rows together to assemble one quarter section.

Quarter Section Assembly Diagram

2. Repeat Step 1 to make the remaining quarter sections of the quilt top center. Press the seam allowances joining the Rows in the same direction. Press 2 quarter sections upward; press 2 quarter sections downward.
3. Sew quarter sections together.

ADDING BORDERS

1. Follow **Adding Squared Borders**, page 86, to add **side**, then **top** and **bottom inner borders**. Press seam allowances toward the borders.
2. Add **outer borders** in same manner. Press seam allowances toward the borders.

QUILTING AND BINDING

1. Follow **Quilting**, page 86, to mark, layer, and quilt. My quilt is machine quilted with meandering swirls.
2. Follow **Making Templates**, page 82, to make templates using patterns, pages 80-81.
3. For corner scallop, draw an "imaginary" line from the corner of the inner border to the corner of the quilt top. Placing dashed line on template on "imaginary" line on quilt top, use corner template and mark along edge of template. Mark remaining corners in same manner.
4. Referring to photo, draw "imaginary" lines from the seamlines at each "valley" to the edge of the borders; mark each "valley" at edge of borders.
5. Beginning at corner and working toward center of each border and using side scallop template, mark along "valley" of scallop template.
6. Trim quilt top along drawn lines.
7. Cut a 22" x 22" square from fabric for binding. Follow **Making Continuous Bias Strip Binding**, page 90, Steps 1-7, to make 320" of 1$^{1}/_{4}$"w bias binding. Follow **Binding Scalloped Edges**, page 95, to bind quilt.

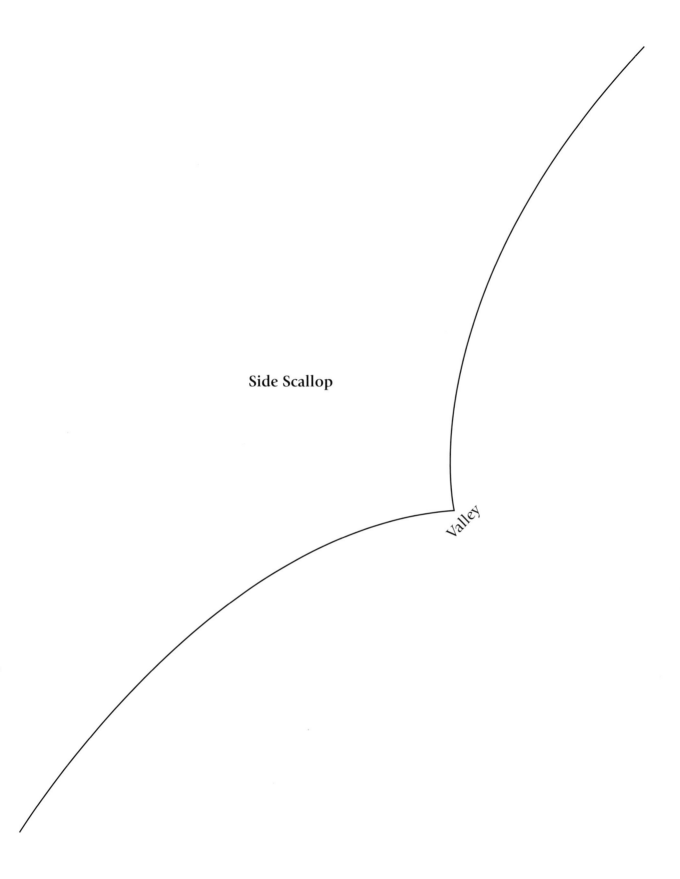

Side Scallop

Valley

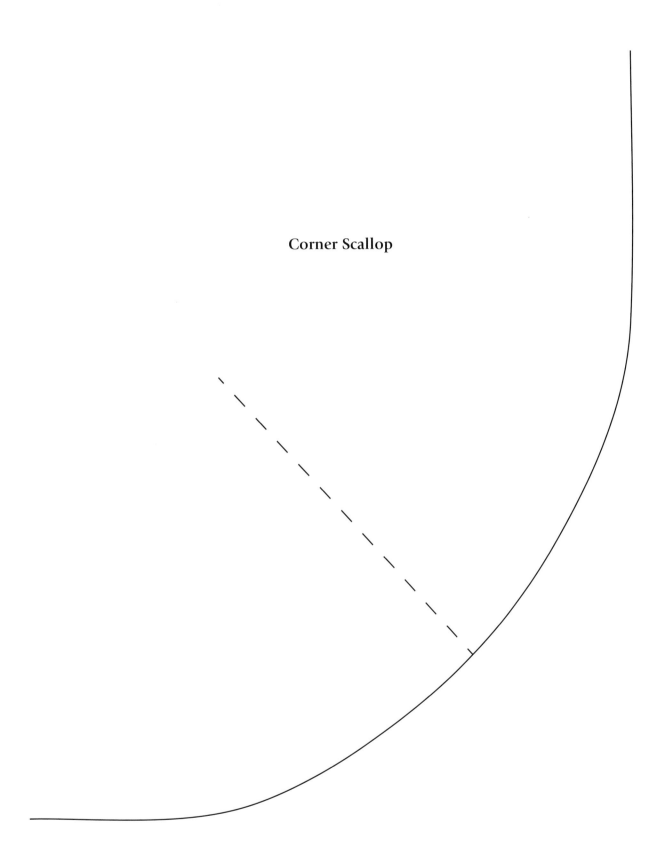

Corner Scallop

General
instructions

To make your quilting easier and more enjoyable, we encourage you to carefully read all of the general instructions, study the color photographs, and familiarize yourself with the individual project instructions before beginning a project.

FABRICS
SELECTING FABRICS

Choose high-quality, medium-weight 100% cotton fabrics. All-cotton fabrics hold a crease better, fray less, and are easier to quilt than cotton/polyester blends.

Yardage requirements listed for each project are based on 43"/44" wide fabric with a "usable" width of 40" after shrinkage and trimming selvages. Actual usable width will probably vary slightly from fabric to fabric. Our recommended yardage lengths should be adequate for occasional re-squaring of fabric when many cuts are required.

While the size of fat quarters may vary slightly, each should be at least 18" x 22" (46 cm x 56 cm). If they are smaller, more fat quarters may be required.

PREPARING FABRICS

We do not recommend pre-washing your yardage, fat quarters, jelly rolls, or charm squares. Pre-washing fabrics may cause edges to ravel. As a result, your fat quarters may not be large enough to cut all of the pieces required for your chosen project and your jelly roll strips and charm squares may be too small. Refer to **Caring for Your Quilt**, page 96, for instructions on washing your finished quilt.

Before cutting, prepare fabrics with a steam iron set on cotton and starch or sizing (such as Best Press™ sizing/Clear Starch Alternative). The starch or sizing will give the fabric a crisp finish. This will make cutting more accurate and may make piecing easier.

When using charm squares, occasionally in the manufacturing process a piece will get a fold or crimp in it. If needed, carefully press these pieces and square them to match your other charm squares.

MAKING TEMPLATES

1. Use a permanent fine-point pen to carefully trace pattern onto template plastic, making sure to transfer any alignment markings.
2. Cut out template along inner edge of drawn line. Check template against original pattern for accuracy.

ROTARY CUTTING

Rotary cutting brings speed and accuracy to quiltmaking by allowing quilters to easily cut strips of fabric and then cut those strips into smaller pieces.

CUTTING FROM YARDAGE

- Place fabric on work surface with fold closest to you.
- Cut all strips from the selvage-to-selvage width of the fabric unless otherwise indicated in project instructions.
- Square left edge of fabric using rotary cutter and rulers (**Figs. 1 - 2**).

Fig. 1

Fig. 2

- To cut each strip required for a project, place ruler over cut edge of fabric, aligning desired marking on ruler with cut edge; make cut (**Fig. 3**).

Fig. 3

- When cutting several strips from a single piece of fabric, it is important to make sure that cuts remain at a perfect right angle to the fold; square fabric as needed.

CUTTING FROM FAT QUARTERS

- Place fabric flat on work surface with lengthwise grain (18" edge) closest to you.

- Square fat quarter along the long (22") edge in the same manner as when cutting from yardage.

- Cut all strips parallel to 22" edge of the fabric unless otherwise indicated in project instructions.

- To cut each strip required for a project, place ruler over left edge of fabric, aligning desired marking on ruler with left edge; make cut.

A few tips from *Cardiff Farms*:

The more accurate the cutting and the better the pressing, the easier the pieces will go together and the nicer your finished product will look.

Remember seam allowances are included in all cutting measurements, so cut as directed.

Press your fabric carefully before cutting, removing all folds and wrinkles.

Always begin cutting a new piece of fabric by squaring the edge you will be measuring from.

Last but not least - measure twice and cut once.

Spending a few extra minutes on these steps will help you produce a much nicer finished product.

MACHINE PIECING

- Set sewing machine stitch length for approximately 11 stitches per inch.

- Use neutral-colored general-purpose sewing thread (not quilting thread) in needle and in bobbin.

- An accurate ¹/₄" seam allowance is *essential*. Presser feet that are ¹/₄" wide are available for most sewing machines.

A tip from *Cardiff Farms*:

Use a scant ¹/₄" seam allowance (just a thread smaller than ¹/₄") on all seams. Check your seam allowances. If they are wider than ¹/₄" your block will finish smaller than it should. The more seams in a block, the smaller the block will get.

To check your seam allowance:
Sew two 1¹/₂" x 1¹/₂" pieces together along one side. Open and press from the right side of the fabric. When pressed, this piece should measure 1¹/₂" x 2¹/₂". If the piece does not measure 2¹/₂", adjust your stitching line. If needed, mark a guide on your sewing machine with tape or mole skin.

- When piecing, always place pieces right sides together and match raw edges; pin if necessary.

- Trim away points of seam allowances that extend beyond edges of sewn pieces.

SEWING STRIP SETS

When there are several strips to assemble into a strip set, first sew strips together into pairs, then sew pairs together to form the strip set. To help avoid distortion, sew seams in opposite directions (**Fig. 4**). Press all seam allowances in one direction.

Fig. 4

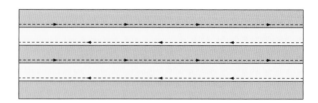

SEWING ACROSS SEAM INTERSECTIONS

When sewing across intersection of two seams, place pieces right sides together and "lock" seams together exactly, making sure seam allowances are pressed in opposite directions (**Fig. 5**).

Fig. 5

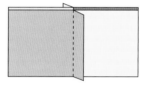

SEWING SHARP POINTS

To ensure sharp points when joining triangular or diagonal pieces, stitch across the center of the "X" (shown in pink) formed on wrong side by previous seams (**Fig. 6**).

Fig. 6

CHAIN PIECING

Chain piecing saves time and will usually result in more accurate piecing. Stack the pieces you will be sewing beside your machine in the order you will need them and in a position that will allow you to easily pick them up. Pick up each pair of pieces, carefully place them together as they will be sewn, and feed them into the machine one after the other. Stop between each pair only long enough to pick up the next, and don't cut thread between pairs (**Fig. 7**). After all pieces are sewn, cut threads, press, and go on to the next step, chain piecing when possible.

Fig. 7

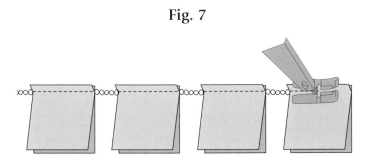

PRESSING

- Use steam iron set on "Cotton" for all pressing.

- Press after sewing each seam.

- To prevent dark fabric seam allowance from showing through light fabric, trim darker seam allowance slightly narrower than lighter seam allowance.

- To press long seams, such as those in long strip sets, without curving or other distortion, lay strips across width of the ironing board.

A few tips from *Cardiff Farms*:

Remember pressing is different than ironing. Pressing is applying heat and pressure to a piece without the back and forth motion of ironing. The back and forth motion along with heat from the iron can distort your fabric and cause your piece to measure the wrong size.

Unless otherwise noted, press seam allowances in the direction that will create the least amount of bulk and whenever possible, toward the darker fabric.

First, set the seam. After determining which fabric the seam allowances will be pressed toward, place the piece on the ironing board with that fabric facing up. Give the closed piece a short press.

Starting in the middle and working your way to each end, press along the seam on the right side of your fabrics. Be careful not to apply too much pressure. This can distort the fabric. When fully open, give one last press to flatten. This will open your seam without leaving any folds or pleats on the front of your quilt which can get caught in later seams.

When sewing Blocks together to make Rows, press seam allowances on all even numbered Rows in one direction and seam allowances on all odd numbered Rows in the opposite direction.

ADDING SQUARED BORDERS

In most cases, our instructions for cutting borders include an extra 2" of length at each end for "insurance;" borders will be trimmed after measuring completed center section of quilt top.

1. Mark the center of each edge of quilt top.
2. Squared borders are usually added to sides, then top and bottom edges of the quilt top center. To add side borders, lay quilt top center on a flat surface; measure across quilt top center to determine length of borders (**Fig. 8**). Trim side borders to the determined length.

Fig. 8

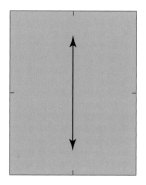

3. Mark center of 1 long edge of each side border. Matching center marks and raw edges, pin borders to quilt top, easing in any fullness; stitch. Press seam allowances toward the borders.

4. Measure across center of quilt top, including attached borders, to determine length of top and bottom borders. Trim top/bottom borders to the determined length. Repeat Step 3 to add borders to quilt top (**Fig. 9**).

Fig. 9

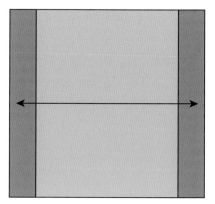

QUILTING

*Quilting holds the three layers (top, batting, and backing) of the quilt together and can be done by hand or machine. Because marking, layering, and quilting are interrelated and may be done in different orders depending on circumstances, please read entire **Quilting** section, pages 86 – 89, before beginning project.*

TYPES OF QUILTING DESIGNS
In the Ditch Quilting
Quilting along seamlines or along edges of appliquéd pieces is called "in the ditch" quilting. This type of quilting should be done on side **opposite** seam allowance and does not have to be marked.

Outline Quilting
Quilting a consistent distance, usually ¹/₄", from seam or appliqué is called "outline" quilting. Outline quilting may be marked, or ¹/₄" wide masking tape may be placed along seamlines for quilting guide. (Do not leave tape on quilt longer than necessary, since it may leave an adhesive residue.)

Motif Quilting

Quilting a design, such as a feathered wreath, is called "motif" quilting. This type of quilting should be marked before basting quilt layers together.

Echo Quilting

Quilting that follows the outline of an appliquéd or pieced design with two or more parallel lines is called "echo" quilting. This type of quilting does not need to be marked.

Channel Quilting

Quilting with straight, parallel lines is called "channel" quilting. This type of quilting may be marked or stitched using a guide.

Crosshatch Quilting

Quilting straight lines in a grid pattern is called "crosshatch" quilting. Lines may be stitched parallel to edges of quilt or stitched diagonally. This type of quilting may be marked or stitched using a guide.

Meandering Quilting

Quilting in random curved lines and swirls is called "meandering" quilting. Quilting lines should not cross or touch each other. This type of quilting does not need to be marked.

Stipple Quilting

Meandering quilting that is very closely spaced is called "stipple" quilting. Stippling will flatten the area quilted and is often stitched in background areas to raise appliquéd or pieced designs. This type of quilting does not need to be marked.

MARKING QUILTING LINES

Quilting lines may be marked using fabric marking pencils, chalk markers, water- or air-soluble pens, or lead pencils.

Simple quilting designs may be marked with chalk or chalk pencil after basting. A small area may be marked, then quilted, before moving to next area to be marked. Intricate designs should be marked before basting using a more durable marker.

Caution: Pressing may permanently set some marks. **Test** different markers **on scrap fabric** to find one that marks clearly and can be thoroughly removed.

A wide variety of pre-cut quilting stencils, as well as entire books of quilting patterns, are available. Using a stencil makes it easier to mark intricate or repetitive designs.

To make a stencil from a pattern, center template plastic over pattern and use a permanent marker to trace pattern onto plastic. Use a craft knife with single or double blade to cut channels along traced lines (**Fig. 10**).

Fig. 10

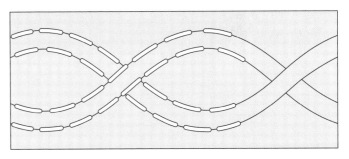

PREPARING THE BACKING

To allow for slight shifting of quilt top during quilting, backing should be approximately 4" larger on all sides. Yardage requirements listed for quilt backings are calculated for 43"/44"w fabric. Using 90"w or 108"w fabric for the backing of a bed-sized quilt may eliminate piecing. To piece a backing using 43"/44"w fabric, use the following instructions.

1. Measure length and width of quilt top; add 8" to each measurement.
2. If determined width is 79" or less, cut backing fabric into two lengths slightly longer than determined *length* measurement. Trim selvages. Place lengths with right sides facing and sew long edges together, forming tube (**Fig. 11**). Match seams and press along one fold (**Fig. 12**). Cut along pressed fold to form single piece (**Fig. 13**).

Fig. 11	**Fig. 12**	**Fig. 13**

3. If determined width is more than 79", it may require less fabric yardage if the backing is pieced horizontally. Divide determined *length* measurement by 40" to determine how many widths will be needed. Cut required number of widths the determined *width* measurement. Trim selvages. Sew long edges together to form single piece.
4. Trim backing to size determined in Step 1; press seam allowances open.

CHOOSING THE BATTING

The appropriate batting will make quilting easier. For fine hand quilting, choose low-loft batting. All cotton or cotton/polyester blend battings work well for machine quilting because the cotton helps "grip" quilt layers. If quilt is to be tied, a high-loft batting, sometimes called extra-loft or fat batting, may be used to make quilt "fluffy."

Types of batting include cotton, polyester, wool, cotton/polyester blend, cotton/wool blend, and silk.

When selecting batting, refer to package labels for characteristics and care instructions. Cut batting same size as prepared backing.

ASSEMBLING THE QUILT

1. Examine wrong side of quilt top closely; trim any seam allowances and clip any threads that may show through front of the quilt. Press quilt top, being careful not to "set" any marked quilting lines.
2. Place backing *wrong* side up on flat surface. Use masking tape to tape edges of backing to surface. Place batting on top of backing fabric. Smooth batting gently, being careful not to stretch or tear. Center quilt top *right* side up on batting.
3. Use 1" rustproof safety pins to "pin-baste" all layers together, spacing pins approximately 4" apart. Begin at center and work toward outer edges to secure all layers. If possible, place pins away from areas that will be quilted, although pins may be removed as needed when quilting.

MACHINE QUILTING METHODS

Use general-purpose thread in bobbin. Do not use quilting thread. Thread the needle of machine with general-purpose thread or transparent monofilament thread to make quilting blend with quilt top fabrics. Use decorative thread, such as a metallic or contrasting-color general-purpose thread, to make quilting lines stand out more.

Straight-Line Quilting

The term "straight-line" is somewhat deceptive, since curves (especially gentle ones) as well as straight lines can be stitched with this technique.

1. Set stitch length for six to ten stitches per inch and attach walking foot to sewing machine.
2. Determine which section of quilt will have longest continuous quilting line, oftentimes the area from center top to center bottom. Roll up and secure each edge of quilt to help reduce the bulk, keeping fabrics smooth. Smaller projects may not need to be rolled.
3. Begin stitching on longest quilting line, using very short stitches for the first $1/4$" to "lock" quilting. Stitch across project, using one hand on each side of walking foot to slightly spread fabric and to guide fabric through machine. Lock stitches at end of quilting line.
4. Continue machine quilting, stitching longer quilting lines first to stabilize quilt before moving on to other areas.

Free-Motion Quilting

Free-motion quilting may be free form or may follow a marked pattern.

1. Attach a darning foot to sewing machine and lower or cover feed dogs.
2. Position quilt under darning foot; lower foot. Holding top thread, take a stitch and pull bobbin thread to top of quilt. To "lock" beginning of quilting line, hold top and bobbin threads while making three to five stitches in place.
3. Use one hand on each side of the darning foot to slightly spread fabric and to move fabric through the machine. Even stitch length is achieved by using smooth, flowing hand motion and steady machine speed. Slow machine speed and fast hand movement will create long stitches. Fast machine speed and slow hand movement will create short stitches. Move quilt sideways, back and forth, in a circular motion, or in a random motion to create desired designs; do not rotate quilt. Lock stitches at end of each quilting line.

MAKING A HANGING SLEEVE

Attaching a hanging sleeve to back of wall hanging or quilt before the binding is added allows project to be displayed on wall.

1. Measure width of quilt top edge and subtract 1". Cut piece of fabric 7"w by determined measurement.
2. Press short edges of fabric piece $^1/_4$" to wrong side; press edges $^1/_4$" to wrong side again and machine stitch in place.
3. Matching wrong sides, fold piece in half lengthwise to form tube.
4. Follow project instructions to sew binding to quilt top and to trim backing and batting. Before Blindstitching binding to backing, match raw edges and stitch hanging sleeve to center top edge on back of quilt.
5. Finish binding quilt, treating hanging sleeve as part of backing.
6. Blindstitch bottom of hanging sleeve to backing, taking care not to stitch through to front of quilt.
7. Insert a dowel or slat into hanging sleeve.

BINDING

Binding encloses the raw edges of quilt. Because of its stretchiness, bias binding works well for binding projects with curves or rounded corners and tends to lie smooth and flat in any given circumstance. Binding may also be cut from straight lengthwise or crosswise grain of fabric.

MAKING CONTINUOUS BIAS STRIP BINDING

Bias strips for binding can simply be cut and pieced to desired length. However, when a long length of binding is needed, the "continuous" method is quick and accurate.

1. Cut square from binding fabric the size indicated in project instructions. Cut square in half diagonally to make two triangles.
2. With right sides together and using $^1/_4$" seam allowance, sew triangles together (**Fig. 14**); press seam allowances open.

Fig. 14

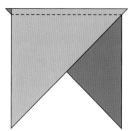

3. On wrong side of fabric, draw lines the width of binding as specified in project instructions (**Fig. 15**). Cut off any remaining fabric less than this width.

Fig. 15

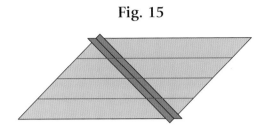

4. With right sides inside, bring short edges together to form tube; match raw edges so that first drawn line of top section meets second drawn line of bottom section (**Fig. 16**).

Fig. 16

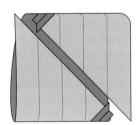

5. Carefully pin edges together by inserting pins through drawn lines at point where drawn lines intersect, making sure pins go through intersections on both sides. Using ¹/₄" seam allowance, sew edges together; press seam allowances open.

6. To cut continuous strip, begin cutting along first drawn line (**Fig. 17**). Continue cutting along drawn line around tube.

Fig. 17

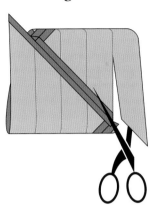

7. Trim ends of bias strip square.
8. Matching wrong sides and raw edges, carefully press bias strip in half lengthwise to complete binding.

MAKING STRAIGHT-GRAIN BINDING

1. Using diagonal seams (**Fig. 18**), sew binding strips together end to end to make 1 continuous binding strip.

Fig. 18

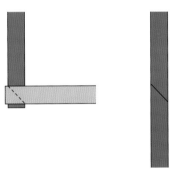

2. Matching wrong sides and raw edges, press strip in half lengthwise.

ATTACHING BINDING WITH MITERED CORNERS

1. Beginning with one end near center on bottom edge of quilt, lay binding around quilt to make sure that seams in binding will not end up at a corner. Adjust placement if necessary. Matching raw edges of binding to raw edge of quilt top, pin binding to right side of quilt along one edge.

2. When you reach first corner, mark ¹/₄" from corner of quilt top (**Fig. 19**).

Fig. 19

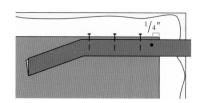

3. Beginning approximately 10" from end of binding and using ¹/₄" seam allowance, sew binding to quilt, backstitching at beginning of stitching and at mark (**Fig. 20**). Lift needle out of fabric and clip thread.

Fig. 20

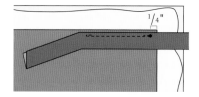

4. Fold binding as shown in **Figs. 21 – 22** and pin binding to adjacent side, matching raw edges. When you've reached the next corner, mark ¹/₄" from edge of quilt top.

Fig. 21

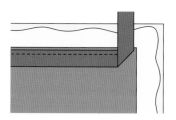

Fig. 22

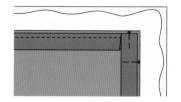

5. Backstitching at edge of quilt top, sew pinned binding to quilt (**Fig. 23**); backstitch at the next mark. Lift needle out of fabric and clip thread.

Fig. 23

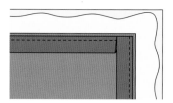

6.	Continue sewing binding to quilt, stopping approximately 10" from starting point (**Fig. 24**).

Fig. 24

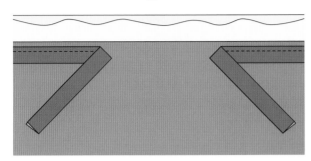

7.	Bring beginning and end of binding to center of opening and fold each end back, leaving a $^1/_4$" space between folds (**Fig. 25**). Finger press folds.

Fig. 25

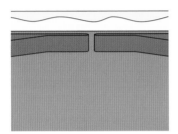

8.	Unfold ends of binding and draw a line across wrong side in finger-pressed crease. Draw a line through the lengthwise pressed fold of binding at the same spot to create a cross mark. With edge of ruler at cross mark, line up 45° angle marking on ruler with one long side of binding. Draw a diagonal line from edge to edge. Repeat on remaining end, making sure that the two diagonal lines are angled the same way (**Fig. 26**).

Fig. 26

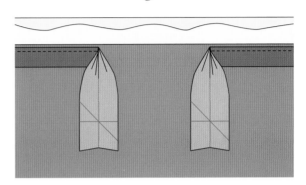

9. Matching right sides and diagonal lines, pin binding ends together at right angles (**Fig. 27**).

Fig. 27

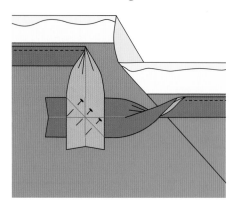

10. Machine stitch along diagonal line (**Fig. 28**), removing pins as you stitch.

Fig. 28

11. Lay binding against quilt to double check that it is correct length.
12. Trim binding ends, leaving ¹/₄" seam allowance; press seam open. Stitch binding to quilt.

13. Trim backing and batting a scant ¹/₄" larger than quilt top so that batting and backing will fill the binding when it is folded over to quilt backing.
14. On one edge of quilt, fold binding over to quilt backing and pin pressed edge in place, covering stitching line (**Fig. 29**). On adjacent side, fold binding over, forming a mitered corner (**Fig. 30**). Repeat to pin remainder of binding in place.

Fig. 29

Fig. 30

15. Blindstitch binding to backing, taking care not to stitch through to front of quilt.

BLIND STITCH

Come up at 1, go down at 2, and come up at 3 (**Fig. 31**). Length of stitches may be varied as desired.

Fig. 31

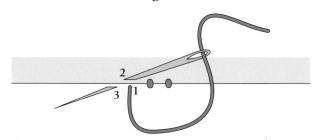

BINDING SCALLOPED EDGES

1. Press 1 short edge and 1 long edge of binding ¹/₄" to wrong side. To sew around scallops, pin binding to 1 scallop at a time as you sew. Gently ease binding around outer curves, being careful not to stretch binding. At points of "valleys," raise presser foot to turn the corner, keeping the fabric as smooth as possible.
2. Trim batting and backing even with quilt top.
3. Blindstitch binding to quilt backing, folding binding at "valleys" to miter as needed.

SIGNING AND DATING YOUR QUILT

A completed quilt is a work of art and should be signed and dated. There are many different ways to do this and numerous books on the subject. The label should reflect the style of the quilt, the occasion or person for which it was made, and the quilter's own particular talents. Following are suggestions for recording the history of quilt or adding a sentiment for future generations.

- Embroider quilter's name, date, and any additional information on quilt top or backing. Matching floss, such as cream floss on white border, will leave a subtle record. Bright or contrasting floss will make the information stand out.

- Make label from muslin and use permanent marker to write information. Use different colored permanent markers to make label more decorative. Stitch label to back of quilt.

- Use photo-transfer paper to add image to white or cream fabric label. Stitch label to back of quilt.

- Piece an extra block from quilt top pattern to use as label. Add information with permanent fabric pen. Appliqué block to back of quilt.

- Write message on appliquéd design from quilt top. Attach appliqué to back of the quilt.

CARING FOR YOUR QUILT

- Wash finished quilt in cold water on gentle cycle with mild soap. Soaps such as Orvus® Paste or Charlie's Soap®, which have no softeners, fragrances, whiteners, or other additives, are safest. Rinse twice in cold water.

- Use a dye magnet, such as Shout® Color Catcher®, each time the quilt is washed to absorb any dyes that bleed. When washing quilt the first time, you may choose to use two color catchers for extra caution.

- Dry quilt on low heat/air fluff in 15 minute increments until dry.

Metric Conversion Chart

Inches x 2.54 = centimeters (cm)		Yards x .9144 = meters (m)
Inches x 25.4 = millimeters (mm)		Yards x 91.44 = centimeters (cm)
Inches x .0254 = meters (m)		Centimeters x .3937 = inches (")
		Meters x 1.0936 = yards (yd)

Standard Equivalents

1/8"	3.2 mm	0.32 cm	1/8 yard	11.43 cm	0.11 m
1/4"	6.35 mm	0.635 cm	1/4 yard	22.86 cm	0.23 m
3/8"	9.5 mm	0.95 cm	3/8 yard	34.29 cm	0.34 m
1/2"	12.7 mm	1.27 cm	1/2 yard	45.72 cm	0.46 m
5/8"	15.9 mm	1.59 cm	5/8 yard	57.15 cm	0.57 m
3/4"	19.1 mm	1.91 cm	3/4 yard	68.58 cm	0.69 m
7/8"	22.2 mm	2.22 cm	7/8 yard	80 cm	0.8 m
1"	25.4 mm	2.54 cm	1 yard	91.44 cm	0.91 m